Street Wisdom

Connecting with God in Everyday Life

STREET WISDOM

Connecting with God in Everyday Life

ALBERT HOLTZ, OSB

TWENTY-THIRD PUBLICATIONS

185 WILLOW STREET • PO BOX 180 • MYSTIC, CT 06355
TEL: 1-800-321-0411 • FAX: 1-800-572-0788
Bayard E-MAIL: ttpubs@aol.com • www.twentythirdpublications.com

Twenty-Third Publications
A Division of Bayard
185 Willow Street
P.O. Box 180
Mystic, CT 06355
(860) 536-2611 or (800) 321-0411
www.twentythirdpublications.com
ISBN:1-58595-294-X

Library of Congress Catalog Card Number: 2003108556
Printed in the U.S.A.

Contents

IV. Keep Heading Homeward

Introduction

Think twice before tossing that empty bottle over the side the next time you go boating at the seashore.

A discarded bottle lying on the ocean bottom is, it seems, an irresistible temptation for a baby crab. The little creature, about the size of your thumbnail, glides easily through the bottle's mouth to discover an enclosed world that offers everything it needs: plenty of organic debris to eat, shelter from strong currents, and, best of all, protection from the countless predators who feed on young crabs. Delighted, it makes itself at home, and begins to thrive in the cozy surroundings. After some weeks, however, when instinct tells it the time has come to migrate, it crawls confidently to the opening, expecting to swim back out the way it came in. That's when it discovers the ghastly price of that time of perfect security: it's grown too big to fit through the neck of the bottle! In a terrible ironic twist, that safe shelter now becomes a death chamber; its protective shield will be its coffin.

In every human being there is a tension between the lure of the safe and certain on the one hand, and the challenge of the unknown and risky on the other. Our lives are shaped by the ebb and flow of the struggle between these two forces inside us. In this book I call them "mastery" and "intimacy."

Although these words have commonly accepted meanings, I use each of them in a wider sense, contrasting them with one another. Here are a just few of the main differences between the two.

Mastery is the approach to life in which I impose my will on situations and people, using my power to make things happen just the way I want. Intimacy, on the other hand, means the willingness to deal with what is given, without having to change every situation to suit me or to fix what's "wrong" with every person I meet.

Mastery is the part of me that prizes predictability. Mastery hates mystery, because to call something a mystery is to admit that I can't control it. Intimacy, on the other hand, is my instinctive sense that anything worthwhile involves uncertainty and risk. It's what prompts me to tell someone "I love you!" even though there's the chance that he or she will laugh in my face.

Mastery knows only that narrow, external world where I evaluate myself and others in terms of clear, measurable standards. Intimacy, however, finds the ultimate meaning of my life in the realm of inner reality infinitely beyond all my measuring, comparing, and competing.

Mastery is all about me: I use my power and my talents to accomplish my tasks and achieve my goals. Intimacy, by definition, is about us, and involves me in the needs and wants of someone else. Real happiness, according to this approach, comes from relating to and connecting with others, rather than from being absorbed with myself first.

When developmental psychologists describe normal psychological growth as a process of passing by stages from the self-centeredness of the infant to the cheerful self-giving of the adult, they're saying that psychological maturation is the movement from mastery to intimacy.

The dynamic interplay of intimacy and mastery is the main plot of the Bible. God, who is passionately in love with the People of the Covenant, keeps inviting them to risk everything and rely on Yahweh alone, but the Chosen People keep refusing the invitation to divine intimacy, and look for control and security instead in idols, armies, and alliances.

When the Word takes flesh in God's ultimate act of self-revelation, God lays bare the deepest mystery of the Godhead: God is love. This is the underlying theme of this book: since we are made in the image of a God who is love, then our happiness, our freedom, and our very meaning must lie not in power or self-gratification, but self-sacrificing love—in intimacy with God and neighbor.

Jesus left us the gift of the Holy Spirit to work in our hearts and help us lead lives of selfless love. In a culture saturated with control, competition, and consumerism, however, mastery keeps beckoning the way an empty bottle calls to a baby crab, promising a safe citadel with invisible protective walls. *Street Wisdom* is a series of meditations that explores some of the conflicts between mastery and intimacy in my own personal relationships and especially in my life with God.

Every other day I step out the front door of my monastery onto a busy sidewalk in downtown Newark, New Jersey, to go for a brisk stroll. During these one-hour periods the Lord often speaks to me in unexpected places and through some very unlikely people. The following chapters share some insights from these walks. Many of them reflect the wisdom of St. Benedict of Nursia (480-540), whose Rule for Monks I follow as a Benedictine.

Although the reflections may be read in any order, they've been grouped into sections according to four principles of spirituality: "Let Go of Control," "Deal with the Real," "Stay Vulnerable," and "Keep Heading Homeward."

My hope is that this little book's unusual interplay of traditional monastic wisdom and the everyday bustle of city life will offer some useful insights for any modern Christian reader who is trying to recognize and resist the lure of mastery.

May we all respond generously and joyfully each day to the countless invitations of the passionate One who is so ardently seeking each one of us— the God of Intimacy.

Mastery and Intimacy

The chart on the next page includes contrasting pairs of attitudes or behaviors toward yourself and others. At the left end of each line are those more characteristic of mastery, while at the right end are those more characteristic of intimacy. Choose some aspect of your life, such as your work. Go down the pairs, placing a "C" (for "co-workers") on each line at the appropriate spot indicating whether your attitude or behavior toward people at work is closer to one end or the other on that particular scale, or somewhere in the middle. For example, if you think you tend to be very controlling with people in your work place, then put a "C" closer to the left end of the top line.

After placing a "C" on each line, go back and do the same thing again with, say, an "S" for "spouse" or "religious superior," or an "F" for "friends," and then maybe a "G" for your relationship with God. Make up your own categories (pupils, children, customers, and so forth).

When you are done, consider these questions:

1. Are you surprised at any of your responses?
2. What patterns emerge as you look at the placement of the letters on the various lines?
3. Are you comfortable with what you see? Did the exercise point out something about yourself that you may wish to change?
4. You might check your answers by showing them to someone who knows you well.

For Reflection

So do not worry and say 'What are we to eat?' or 'What are we to wear?' All these things the pagans seek. Your heavenly father knows that you need them all. But seek first the kingdom of God and his righteousness, and all these things will be given to you besides (Matthew 6:31–33).

This advice flies in the face of modern pragmatism, which tells you to take care of practical concerns first, and then to deal with the kingdom of God. Have you ever tried seeking the kingdom first in some important decision, trusting that the Lord would take care of the practicalities involved? If so, how did it turn out? Did anyone agree with your decision at the time? Is there a situation in your life right now where God may be calling you to this kind of risk?

MASTERY   ## INTIMACY

Control and power: I need to make things and people into what I want them to be.

"Gentle" approach: I accept and work with things and people as they are.

|———————|——————~~F~~|————————S|—————————|————————►|
JK

I demand perfection from myself and others; I want conformity, and I don't like to make exceptions.

I'm OK with imperfections, including my own. I'm comfortable with individual people's differences.

|———————|—————————|————F|———————|S—————|————————►|
JK

I require lots of predictability in order to be comfortable.

I tend toward spontaneity and enjoy being surprised.

|——F——|—————————|—————————|——S——|—————————|————————►|
JK

I put a high value on self-protection and security; I tend toward secrecy and closedness.

I'm able to leave myself vulnerable and am willing to take risks; I tend toward self-disclosure, openness.

|———————|—————————|————————|F—————|———S——|————————►|
JK

I focus on myself: on my wants, my needs.

I focus on others: on their needs, the group's needs.

|———————|———F—S——|—————————|—————————|—————————|————————►|
JK

I aim for effectiveness and efficiency.

I aim for nurturing and beauty.

|———————|——S——|————————|———F——|—————————|————————►|
JK

I rely on the rational: my head; I mistrust or dismiss emotions.

I rely on my feelings: my heart; I respect and value emotions.

|———————|—————————|————————|S————|—————————|————————►|
JK   F

PART ONE

Let Go of Control

1 Monday

A Muslim's Prayer

The Driver's Seat

Here on Branford Place, a few blocks down the hill from the monastery, several Muslim stores sell books, clothing, posters, incense, and oils. This afternoon the curb is lined, as usual, with sidewalk carts offering bean pies, shish kebob, lemonade, incense sticks, and Islamic literature. A woman and her daughter, both with faces veiled in the traditional fashion, step out of the door of an old building that now houses a Muslim school.

Sitting on a high stool several feet away from his curbside cart, a young man leans against a plate glass window. A well-built fellow in a Muslim cap and long, loose white robe, he sits stock still with back straight, eyes closed, and hands lying loosely in his lap forming two little circles with thumbs and forefingers. He seems deep in meditation, radiating a serious intensity and an easy inner peace.

As I walk past I'm struck by the contrast between his quiet meditation and the noisy bustle of the passing traffic. He's on his own island of silence in a sea of sound.

I wish I could pray as easily as that, I say to myself as I stride past him, unnoticed. Actually, sometimes I am able to let down my guard and have a wonderful, deep experience of God's closeness. But more often meditation time is a struggle for me.

9

I used to blame my difficulty with quiet prayer on my very action-oriented personality, which is naturally sensory and extroverted. Recently, though, I've come to admit the true reason for my trouble—it's fear. Whenever intimacy invites me to stop controlling and leave myself vulnerable to another, I get cold feet. I try to spend as little time as possible on the unfamiliar terrain of intimacy, where I can't be in charge and can't easily predict what's going to happen. So my struggle with prayer is a parable of the rest of my life. The same problems of mastery and control that plague my everyday existence stand out in stark clarity when I sit down for a period of quiet meditation. After about five minutes I start to fidget. Then a dozen important things jump to mind, demanding my immediate attention. Finally a little voice whispers, "Hey, let's get out of here! This isn't going anywhere."

A pack of cars comes roaring down Washington Street, four abreast.

An image comes to mind: I'm in the driver's seat, speeding along on my way somewhere. Then the Lord appears beside me: "Hi, Al! Listen, how about switching seats and letting me drive?" I clutch the wheel in panic and break into a cold sweat. "You?" I stammer, "You want to drive? But then what am I supposed to do?" (What I really mean is, "If you're driving, how do I know where I'll wind up? What if you take us someplace I don't want to go?") Maybe the Lord will just let me rest comfortably in the divine embrace for awhile. But there's also the scary possibility that the Almighty Lover may decide instead to lead me into the darkest, deepest depths of my soul, where the fire of passion could sear me and change me forever!

Sooner or later, true prayer demands the same thing that a happy life does: that I move over and let God drive. Prayer is, like my very existence, God's gift, and not my project. Come to think of it, the most satisfying moments of my life and of my prayer have happened when I've managed to let go and simply place myself in God's hands. The strange paradox is that despite those great experiences, I still spend much of my life and my prayer time arguing with God over which of us is going to drive. It's not exactly mystical union, I suppose, but somehow the Lord manages to use even my stubborn cowardice to draw me into a constant and lively dialogue.

I scoot across University Avenue with the yellow light and continue the last two blocks to the monastery. A couple of my students are coming down the sidewalk toward me on their way from school.

"Hey, Fath' Al. 'Sup?"

"Hi, guys! Listen, Brad, make sure you're ready for that test tomorrow."

"I will be. I'm gonna study tonight."

"All right, see you guys in the morning."

"Later, Father."

We continue on our separate ways.

I start to imagine what would happen if I were to live my life the way that Muslim fellow prays—with calm, open intimacy. I would welcome each person I meet with a humble acceptance of who they are and what they are feeling. I would approach every situation, no matter how threatening or unpleasant, with gentle joy, seeing it as a fresh challenge and a new opportunity to grow closer to God. I would come to prayer with no holding back, willing and even eager to be swept into the arms of a passionate God who is sometimes unpredictable but always loving.

I continue my walk up Branford Place humbled by the lesson of that Muslim sitting quietly on his stool. He didn't even see me go by, but I'm grateful to him for reminding me what my prayer and even my whole life could be like if I would just learn to move over and let God drive.

For Reflection

1. What are some areas where you have little or no trouble letting God drive? What particular part of your life do you find most difficult to just hand over to God? Why do you think it's hard for you to let God take the wheel? →use of cabin, how I spend my time, finding the right house →It will be unwelcoming if things aren't planned out.

2. Think of a situation where you overcame your need to have your hands on the steering wheel and were able to let someone else be in charge. Why did you do it? Was it difficult? What did you learn from the experience? →to help girls gain independence that people still ask me if that the wife/mom is judged.

3. In Psalm 31 the psalmist describes both his misery and his unshaken confidence in God's goodness. Try reading the whole psalm. Feel the intimacy and confidence that underlies the psalmist's phrase uttered in the midst of overwhelming danger and distress: "Into your hands I commend my spirit, you will redeem me, O Lord, faithful God" (Psalm 31:6). This is the prayer that Jesus utters as he dies on the cross (Luke 23:46). Think of a situation in your own life that evokes a similar feeling of helplessness, and try praying this same little prayer of trust.

2 _Tuesday_

Douglas

My Two-Year-Old

The electric sliding doors of the Rite-Aid Pharmacy have barely parted when a young mother charges out onto Washington Street tugging a two-year-old in a dark blue Yankees jacket and matching cap. He's tugging right back, pointing behind him to the store and whimpering in protest. I have the impression that this has been going on for some minutes, and that Mom, who's obviously in a hurry to get somewhere, is running out of patience. And so is he, as he pulls harder and harder, his gaze still riveted behind him. She is now peering intently down Market Street, hoping, no doubt, to see her bus coming.

Just as I stop beside them at the corner of Market Street, he explodes into a loud, outraged wail. This, I think to myself, is the very picture of the terrible twos.

He's making the awful discovery each of us makes at his age: you can't always get everything you want. The humiliations have started piling up. Maybe yesterday he was at the kitchen table and made a grab for the shiny carving knife but his father snatched it out of his reach. Then, just as his favorite aunt arrived, he got picked up and plunked, kicking and screaming, into his crib for a nap. Just two minutes ago in the store he told Mommy he wanted a Pokémon toy and she simply answered, "No, not today," and then pulled him through the exit and onto the street where we are now. You could

13

say that he is discovering the basic but devastating truth that he is not God.
This little fellow's discovery process is in full swing here on the sidewalk.
As I watch out of the corner of my eye, he lets his knees go perfectly limp,
forcing his mother to hold him up by the arm like some oversized rag doll.

You can't blame him for wanting to be God. We're actually made that way,
created in the Yahweh's image and likeness. So we spend our lives mourning
the loss of that divine likeness and trying through our personal God project
to recover it.

Most of us experience the drive to be like God as the desire for limitless
power. We're fascinated by the awesome might of the One who, according
to Psalm 134, can do "whatever he wills, in heaven, on earth, and in the
seas." As we mature in our faith, though, we come to see that there's a lot
more to being like God than simply imposing our own will on the world.
With the help of grace we come to understand that there's really only one
thing we need to know and to imitate about God: that God is love—infinite,
self-sacrificing, unconditional love.

I hope the light changes soon, because Mommy's patience is just about to
snap, and I don't want to be too nearby when it does. She tugs his arm
roughly, "Stand up! Stop that!" He's not about to give up, however, without
at least one more try. He stands bolt upright, throws back his little head, and
lets out a roar of rage. A kindly, gray-haired little woman nods to the harried mother, encouraging her with an eloquent, knowing smile of sisterly
solidarity that says, "Oh yes, honey! It'll be like that for awhile. But don't
worry, he'll grow out of it. All of mine did."

The mature Christian's God project doesn't aim at Godlike mastery over people or events, but at Godlike intimacy with the Lord and others. Jesus, the perfect model of this ideal, led a life of selfless love. "Learn from me, for I am meek
and humble of heart," he tells us, and "There is no greater love than this, to lay
down one's life for one's friend." This is the kind of divinity we're called to—this
is the only worthwhile God project. But to make it happen we need to deal firm-
ly with our inner two-year-old who is always screaming for control and wanting to be, like God, the center of everything and in charge of the world.

The monastic life is designed to unmask our two-year-old and keep our
false self in check through the discipline of common ownership of goods,
the asking of simple permissions, community life, restraint of speech, fast-
ing, and other practices.

"Douglas Michael, you just cut that out!"

People standing at the bus stop look on poker-faced as the frustrated mother continues.

"You hear me, boy? I already told you, no Pokémon, and that's it! You keep carrying on, I'm gonna give you something to cry about!"

I'm not exactly sure why, but something about this scene is making me very uneasy. As soon as the light changes I dart onto the crosswalk leaving little Douglas still tugging at his mother's hand.

By the time I reach the other curb I think I've figured out why this little drama has unnerved me: as I watched Douglas doing his little power plays back there, I got the eerie feeling that I was watching myself in a mirror!

The self-centered two-year-old inside me has been pushing me around

pretty persistently lately, trying to run the show. It's been hard for me to say no to a piece of candy or dessert—a little voice inside keeps screaming, "But I want it!" Just this morning my own version of little Douglas abruptly cut off a discussion with a brother instead of hearing him out, because my Godlike control of the situation seemed threatened.

What must my relationship with God look like from the Lord's point of view? Do I have the spirituality of a poorly behaved two-year-old? Suddenly a picture flashes in front of my mind's eye, an image from Isaiah: "As a mother comforts her son, so will I comfort you" (Isaiah 66:13). God is suddenly my patient young mother bending over me and offering me her help. I stomp my little foot and shout, "No! I can do it myself!" Then she asks me to do something that I find distasteful and I whine, "No! I don't want to. I won't!" When she tries to coax me to risk reaching out in love to someone in need, I whimper, "No! I can't! I'm scared!"

Yet, just like any loving mother, she still keeps coaxing, cajoling, and reassuring me all the time. She's confident that one day, I'll grow out of this mastery stage and mature into a joyful incarnation of intimacy, another Christ.

I resist the urge to glance back toward the bus stop to see if Douglas has given in.

For Reflection

1. Did Douglas's behavior remind you of parts of yourself? "When I was a child I used to talk like a child, think like a child, reason like a child. But when I became a man I put childish ways aside" (1 Corinthians 13:11). If your own inner two-year-old were to mature, how might that show itself in your actions or words? What people might benefit most from such a change in you? *My husband, my co-volunteers, my daughters*

2. Do you have a personal God project of holding on to control and power in certain areas of your life? If so, how does it affect your relationships with others? With God? *→ In my volunteering. In my family.*
   ↳ w/ others is at arms length, so that I don't feel it necessary to hear everything about them,
   ↳ w/ God keeps me from fully seeing what at work in the world by because I don't slow down and look for them,

Bridge Street

The Gentle Life

I'm still a block away when I hear the first loud clang of the warning bell. I look at my watch. Oh brother! This is gonna be close!

At the end of Harrison Avenue white-and-red-striped barriers slowly drop into place, blocking traffic onto the Bridge Street bridge. On the other side of the Passaic River stands the skyline of Newark.

I left later than usual for my walk, and now this interruption is probably going to make me late for five o'clock Mass. The first car pulls to a stop at the gates. Keeping my quick pace, I stride up to the little barrier that blocks the sidewalk and stand staring at the bridge's superstructure, a forest of gray steel Xs, Zs and Vs. No sign of a ship anywhere.

The red lights of the gates blink on and off, on and off, slowly, calmly, as if taunting the half dozen cars that are waiting impatiently to cross the bridge. Somewhere behind me a driver blows his horn loudly in protest. I glance over my shoulder to see a car peel out of the line in a screeching U-turn and race back the way it came, probably heading over to the Stickel Bridge to cross there. A moment later two others follow its lead. I turn back to look at the bridge.

At last the gray steel skeleton starts to revolve, slowly and silently, pivoting around its center like a giant turnstile. The cement sidewalk in front of me swings out of the way, leaving nothing but empty space in its place. The reality of my situation now strikes me: late or not, I have no alternative but to stand here helpless, waiting for the bridge to swing back again.

I notice the third car in line, a red Honda. A young woman is sitting at the steering wheel calmly reading a paperback. It occurs to me that she probably has the right approach.

There are times when some event gets in the way of your plans and there is nothing you can do to change the situation. Sure, you can get upset, you can fume, you can shout at everybody within earshot, but you can't really alter the fact that your plans will have to change.

It's possible, though, to take what Father Adrian Van Kaam calls the "gentle" approach: you admit that you can't control the undesirable situation, you accept it as a given, and then make the best of it. If you're stuck behind a hay wagon on a back road, you take advantage of the delay to appreciate the wildflowers along the roadside that you'd never have noticed otherwise.

Well, there's nothing I can do about the bridge, so I decide to take the opportunity to just relax for a few minutes. I notice the ragged edges of clouds against the pale blue sky and feel the cool spring breeze on my face. Down to my left, on the opposite bank, I imagine Robert Treat and his little band of Puritans stepping ashore in 1666, full of hope in God as they began to carve a new town out of the woods. The deep throbbing of a ship's engine starts to rumble in from the right.

Benedict himself has this gentleness thing down pretty well. In Chapter 49 of the Rule, "The Observance of Lent," he says "The life of a monk ought to be a continuous Lent. Since few, however, have the strength for this, we urge the entire community during these days of Lent to keep its manner of life most pure." In Chapter 40, "The Proper Amount of Drink," he concedes, "We read that monks should not drink wine at all, but since the monks of our day cannot be convinced of this, let us at least agree to drink moderately, and not to the point of excess." In Chapter 64, "The Election of an Abbot," he warns the abbot not to be overly enthusiastic in his efforts to fix people, but to "use prudence and avoid extremes; otherwise by rubbing too hard to remove the rust, he may break the vessel." Benedict always works with the reality of the human condition and doesn't waste time wishing things were different.

I glance once again at the string of sullen, sulking drivers waiting in frustration for the irritating interruption to end.

Gentleness can become my usual way of responding to situations. In fact it's absolutely necessary for sustaining a healthy relationship. When I really love someone, I take that person just as he or she is, complete with imperfections. Intimacy doesn't need or even want to change the other person. If I first have to fix that person to fit my requirements, then I'm not looking for intimacy but mastery.

Do I really believe, I ask myself, that God loves me without having to fix me first? There are times when it seems impossible that God could love me just the way I am!

Am I able to pass God's love along to others the same way, without having to put conditions on it? Sometimes I lack Benedict's patience with flawed people and imperfect situations, and I try to change my brother monks or my students to fit my wants. It's very easy to forget that my calling as a Christian is to love people just as they are.

The warning bell breaks in on my musing. The rumble of the boat has moved downstream to my left. After seven minutes of interrupting the flow of people's lives, the gates start to lift slowly skyward, their red flashers still blinking peacefully in the afternoon sky.

The first cars charge across the bridge from either end, trying to make up some of the lost time. As the little gate blocking the sidewalk goes up, I manage to keep myself from running—and refuse look at my watch.

For Reflection

1. In Romans 5:8 Paul reminds us that "Christ died for us while we were still sinners." Has anyone ever loved you without being concerned with changing you first? Has anyone ever tried to fix you to that person's specifications? If so, how did you feel about it? Are there people in your life that you're tempted to fix?

2. Under what circumstances do you find it hardest to take a gentle approach? When is it easiest?

3. Do you take a gentle approach with your own imperfections, or are you more tolerant of others' faults than of your own?

4 _Thursday_

The Botanica

Hedging My Bets

Most of the sidewalk conversations are, like the store signs, in Spanish or Portuguese. Ferry Street is one of my favorite places in town, though its crowded sidewalks slow my American power walk to a leisurely Spanish stroll. I pass the *ourivesaria*, its window sparkling with gold necklaces, chains, and earrings. I weave my way among the early-morning shoppers, mostly old women dressed in black squeezing melons and picking over tomatoes at the sidewalk display in front of the grocery shop. The *ferragens* store shows off power tools, packets of sandpaper, and all sorts of gadgets in its window. In a week or so the wine-making equipment will appear out on the sidewalk. I nod at some red-faced men chatting on the pavement in front of a café, then glance at a bank display to check the exchange rate for euros. A couple of travel agencies compete to fly me to Lisbon for the cheapest price. In the tiny *Paõ de Açúcar* there are, as usual, three men sitting at one of its two tables smoking over empty espresso cups. I pause at the window of the fish store to read the Portuguese names on little white plastic signs sticking out of the squid or the strange, metallic-shiny fish. The strong smell of the sea wafts out of the open door while dozens of black eels slither nervously in the big white tub as if they know exactly what the local housewives are planning to do with them this evening.

This August morning I'm out early because the weather forecast is for yet another day of ninety-five degree heat. I find myself stopped in front of the strangest of all the shops. Its window announces in gold letters: *Botanica.*

Since it's not open yet, I can lean against the dusty glass and shade my eyes for a good look deep inside the little shop. There are shelves of candles and oils, each for a specific purpose such as attracting money, finding a lover, or avoiding evil spells. Standing shoulder to shoulder on a counter near the window are foot-high statues of Saint Martin de Porres, a half-naked African woman, the Sacred Heart, an Indian brave, and the Blessed Virgin Mary. When I remember that in Santeria Catholic statues represent various African spirit-gods who borrow the convenient form of Christian saints, a cold, damp draft seems to creep through the plate glass, giving me the chills. Some pretty dark stuff can go on in the back room of a botanica.

On the wall to my left packages of ginseng are stacked on a shelf between a pile of crucifixes and boxes of Saint Christopher medals and scapulars. Nearer the window is a rack featuring books on dreams, lucky numbers, and crystals.

Sitting prominently in the center of the window display this morning is a dusty burlap bag overflowing with strange fist-size tufts of green-brown

evergreen needles. A handwritten sign proclaims that this is the famous flor *de jericó*, or Jericho flower, which is also, the sign says, *la flor del dinero* (the money flower).

Various candles sport hand-lettered Spanish labels: this one for warding off the ill wishes of bad neighbors, that for assuring good luck, another for breaking a relationship. I spot dried herbs that can be used for attracting money, and soaps that can keep a lover faithful or protect an unborn baby.

It occurs to me how different this is from the monastery, where we search for intimacy with God. We try hard to put our lives in God's hands, trusting that the Lord of history will love and care for us constantly, especially in those times and events that are beyond our command or our understanding. This little store is all about something quite different: trying to gain control over the great mysterious powers of the universe and make them subject to me. It promises not intimacy with God but mastery over the hidden forces of the cosmos.

Handwritten notes and printed circulars taped in the window advertise the latest products available: a new shipment of *velas de buena suerte* (good-luck candles), and a booklet for Catholics explaining the magical powers of the Shroud of Turin.

Unable to see farther into the dark shadows, I start to turn away from the window, my curiosity satisfied. Then I notice a note taped to the door. Scribbled in Spanish, it tells the customers that because of the extreme heat forecast for today, the store will be closed all day. Not even a botanica can control a New Jersey heat wave, I say to myself as I continue making my way up Ferry Street.

I don't use flor de jericó or scented oil—I'm too sophisticated for that sort of thing. But sometimes I do lose my nerve while waiting for God's mysterious plan to work itself out, and I take matters into my own hands. There's a part of me that prefers the botanica approach: a variety of pathetic attempts to take over when things are threatening to overwhelm me and the Lord seems to be falling down on the job.

Like most Christians, I have my own personal botanica, well stocked with lots of magical remedies that I can call upon in addition to calling on God. I go there when the Almighty is not helping as quickly or as thoroughly as I want. When I'm not sure that God alone will really be enough for me, I can fill the emptiness inside me with all sorts of other things. I can, for example, try burying myself in some important work until I drop with exhaustion, or pursue selfish pleasures or distractions as if they were those special candles that can make troublesome questions simply disappear.

Because I want to be in complete command of every situation, I avoid leaving myself too vulnerable to other people. That's also why it's hard for me to depend totally on the Lord. Trusting in God becomes, then, not my whole way of life but just one option among many—a crucifix on the shelf between the lucky cologne and the magic bath oil.

The monastic vision challenges me to drop all the magical cures and mumbo-jumbo, and depend on God alone. Cassian calls it "purity of heart." My life ought to be a reminder to every Christian to always be on the lookout for things that seem to offer magical substitutes for God: bodily pleasures, preoccupation with achievement at work, private possessions, social status, or domination over others.

Lord, I mutter as I continue up the street, help me to stay out of the botanica. Teach me to trust you to take care of me. Help me to believe you when you say, "My grace is enough for you," and "Behold, I am with you always, even to the end of time!"

For Reflection

1. In Exodus 20:2–3, the first of the ten commandments that God gives to Moses on Mount Sinai is: "I, the Lord, am your God, who brought you out of the land of Egypt, that place of slavery. You shall not have other Gods besides me." Psalm 86:10 says "For you are great, and you do wondrous deeds; you alone are God." A similar phrase occurs in Isaiah 37:16, and other places, "You alone are God." Walk into your own inner botanica and look at the shelves lined with the remedies you keep there to call on when God is not enough. What do you usually fall back on when God fails to deliver? *education for what I can do* *blame the system*

2. Reflect on Matthew 7:7–11, where Jesus encourages us, "Ask and you shall receive." Are you comfortable with praying to ask favors of God? What do you do, think, or feel when you don't get what you expected? *I feel less comfortable asking favors for myself, but better about asking for others.*

Sad, maybe angry. Then, glad it is over.

5 Friday

Fiber Optic Cable

Inefficient God

I stand at the top of the hill that runs beside the abbey church. Down at the bottom end of William Street I see the tower of Old First Presbyterian Church, rebuilt in 1791. Its parsonage, where Aaron Burr was born in 1756, is gone. As I set out down the steep sidewalk I notice two of those white panel trucks that have been all over town the past several weeks installing fiber optic cable under the city streets.

I read an article recently about fiber optic cables. While one pair of copper wires can carry about 30 telephone calls, an optical fiber can carry up to 1,900 telephone calls at a time. Although fiber optics still has some problems to overcome, sending information in the form of laser light over thousands of miles seems to be the future of telecommunications. A fiber optics system will be able to send the equivalent of an encyclopedia set of information in a single second. Forty million words per second—pretty efficient!

As I walk alongside the soccer field fence, I notice a string of orange cones running down the middle of the street to my right, guiding traffic away from an open manhole.

Our culture is always looking for more efficiency, ways to do more work with fewer resources. The less time, effort and attention you have to invest

25

on a task, the better. Because our great technological civilization depends on efficiency, we've gotten amazingly good at it.

As a culture, though, we aren't quite as successful at personal relationships. This is because love just doesn't fit the criteria of mastery—it plays by different rules. Instead of asking "Is this efficient?" or "Is this effective?," loving intimacy asks questions such as "Is this beautiful?" or "Is this life-giving?" or "Is this good for the other person?"

Lovers spend hours talking to each other about nothing in particular. A healthy family "wastes" time together playing board games or listening to a child's silly riddles. Intimacy requires a huge investment of time and attention with no guarantee of results in return. In short, loving is a pretty inefficient undertaking.

As with any other personal relationship, my life with God will naturally suffer from this same lack of efficiency and effectiveness. The spiritual life eludes mastery's objective measurements and makes light of my worries about getting things done. No wonder so many people think of religious commitment as just about the oddest thing imaginable!

In our age of video teleconferences and cell phones linked to the Internet, communicating with God must be easily the most inefficient activity in the world. First of all, God is painfully shy, and avoids talking to me directly, face to face. The Lord's communication with me is seldom a simple, straightforward process, but usually needs to be carefully discerned and interpreted. For example, I believe that God talks to me through the Scriptures. But after reading a passage I still have to interpret what it means here and now, asking, "How does this apply to me?" I just have to trust that the message I draw from it is the one that the Lord intends.

A second open manhole is protected by a three-sided fence of thin yellow pipes. I'm tempted to walk over and peek down into the dark opening but continue instead down the hill toward the phone building.

God communicates through everyday events as well, they say, and through the people around me. Fine. But the same problem comes up: "What is the Lord's message for me in this stressful situation? Is this a signal that I should quit this job and move on, or is it a test of some sort, challenging me to stick it out right here?" I always have to look prayerfully at an event and ask for the gift of discernment so I can figure out what the Lord wants. Just as in other relationships, no matter how hard I try to listen to

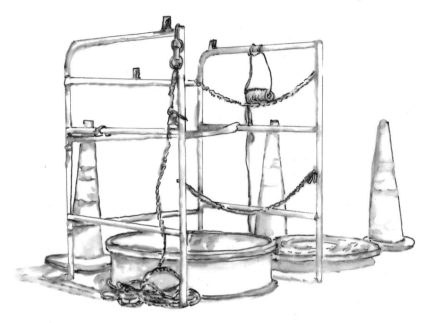

God there's always a risk that I'll misunderstand the message.

All this time-consuming uncertainty, this bothersome ambiguity, is part of God's normal, if terribly inefficient, way of relating with me. Sometimes I get impatient. Why doesn't God save both of us a lot of time and aggravation and just come out and give me the message straight, in plain language? The answer is that God wants to have a close, loving relationship with me—and intimacy always calls for effort, risk, and vulnerability.

I'm alongside the telephone building now. Years ago I took a tour of a couple of its floors, each filled with banks of switches clicking away. Today those noisy old machines have been replaced by silent, super-efficient, high-tech computers.

It's easy to forget how vulnerable God is in this relationship with me. Yahweh created me with a free will so that I'd be able to respond to the divine love with a spontaneous love of my own. Since I'm not programmed to love God (that wouldn't be real love anyway), this means that God is vulnerable to being rejected by me. If now and then I ask God, "Why don't you listen to me?" I have to remember that God is asking me the same question all the time.

There are those who prefer a more predictable, mechanical God who is like, say, a vending machine—you put in the prayers and good works and the Lord automatically delivers some sort of payoff. The customer has a right to complain when the candy machine swallows up his dollar bill without delivering the M&Ms. This is the mentality behind the complaint, "How come God didn't answer my prayers? I kept praying for a special favor, and God didn't come through."

Some people return from Lourdes disillusioned and disappointed with God because the cure they were praying for didn't happen. Others, though, realize that there are many different kinds of healing that bring us closer to God, but which are mysteriously beyond our human perception.

Life becomes both simpler and deeper when I approach God in terms of mystery rather than mastery. Once I stop asking God to play the role of the God of Explanations who owes us mortals a rationale for everything that happens on earth, the Lord can become instead the Tremendous Lover whose mysterious, crazy, passionate ways of loving me are far beyond my ability to fathom. Once I dare to enter the dark cloud of unknowing and leave myself vulnerable to the infinite mystery of God's love, life takes on a depth that can't be described. No matter what troubles or tragedies life presents me with, I live in a joy that nothing and no one can take from me.

As I cross University Avenue I notice telltale symbols spray-painted on the sidewalk and the street pavement. The big letters F.O.C. tell me that more fiber optic cable is about to be buried. We keep getting better and better at communication technology. Too bad life's not just about efficiency.

For Reflection

1. Meditate on Isaiah 55:8–9, "For my thoughts are not your thoughts, nor are your ways my ways, says the Lord." (The entire chapter is a beautiful invitation to grace.) Do you ever feel that God's way of communicating with you is inefficient? Have you ever misinterpreted what you thought God was asking of you? How did you feel when it became evident that you were on the wrong track?

2. Some other passages that express the fact that God's ways are not always clear to us are Job 38:1; Wisdom 9:13; Romans 11:33–35, and 1 Corinthians 2 (the entire chapter). What is your usual response when God asks you to live with so much ambiguity and mystery? Is it grudging acceptance? Impatience? A trusting leap?

PART TWO

Deal with the Real

6 Saturday

The Excavation

Starting with Reality

I wait for a break in the traffic, then trot across Branford Place for a closer view. Last week bulldozers and dump trucks came in, shaved off the asphalt in a day and a half, and began to change a parking lot on Washington Street into this huge hole. It rained last night, and the bottom of the big pit is a mess of deep ruts and tracks, chocolate-colored puddles, and muck. A couple of bulldozers and front-end loaders are sliding around in it like weird yellow reptiles. There's mud all over the place.

It seems that to put up a building you always have to begin in the mud. Actually, lots of things have to start with mud. Even God begins with it, making Adam out of the soil of the earth. Just as a building needs to start in the mud, any kind of human intimacy has to be based on accepting what really and truly is. While mastery over someone can be based merely on force, fear, or lying, intimacy has to be based on the bedrock of truth. I need, for example, to admit and accept my own limits and imperfections, my mud. Then to really love another I need to accept the truth of that person just as he or she really is.

Some Christians think that it's vaguely indecent or at least inappropriate to refer to our mud—especially in the same breath as spirituality. They think that a relationship with God has to be way up in the clouds of some spiritu-

al realm, and has nothing to do with their own very down-to-earth lives.

This tragic misunderstanding of Christian spirituality turns the Gospel right on its head. It's true that our final destiny is a lofty one: a life of eternal intimacy with God in heaven. But the great spiritual masters all agree that in the spiritual life you've got to start where you are. Christian spirituality begins right where this new building is beginning, with the same stuff God started with—mud!

If I want to grow as a person then sooner or later I'll have to get in touch with my own mud by facing the deepest truths about myself. If I want to enjoy real intimacy with anyone—including God—I have to let that other person know my imperfections, so he or she can love me as I really and truly am, a creature made of mud.

It doesn't make any sense, then, to come to prayer all prettied up, trying to look good for God, the one who made me out of mud and who knows me inside out. I have to show up as my real self. It's not God that needs to know the unvarnished truth about me (the Lord already knows everything there is to know). No, the one who really needs to face the truth about myself is me!

Simply getting to this starting point, though, admitting the truth about myself, is a major task in its own right. The first of the twelve steps of Alcoholics Anonymous is often the hardest one of all: "We admitted we were powerless over alcohol, that our lives had become unmanageable."

In one corner of the excavation, huge dump trucks rumble down a long dirt ramp into the pit, pick up a load of dirt, and then labor noisily back up the way they came.

If there are lots of paths that can lead me down to the mud of my life, one of the most useful is Sacred Scripture. Saint Athanasius calls it "a perfect mirror" in which I can look at myself as I truly am. The people and the stories of the Bible can offer me some wonderful grace-filled insights into my own behavior, provided I have the courage to see in them my own reflection. For example, if I look closely at Peter in the courtyard of the high priest's house late on Holy Thursday as he denies that he even knows Jesus, maybe I'll recognize in him my own faintheartedness. Or perhaps watching the poor widow drop her last two pennies into the temple treasury in an act of reckless reliance on Divine Providence will force me to look at my calculating, safe approach to God.

Scripture is only one means the Spirit uses to invite me to face the truth about myself. Another great way to stay in touch with reality is to live in a community—whether in a family, a relationship with a loved one, or in a religious house. I've found that living with my monastic community keeps me in daily touch with my own mud. Shortly after I entered the monastery I began to notice the mud tracks in every hallway and on every stair. My brothers' mud was all over the place! Every one of those guys seemed to be made of the stuff! Then the moments of grace started coming. I began to recognize my own imperfections in the very faults I was complaining about in them. Their loving but sometimes pointed criticisms brought me up short, too, and their well-placed jibes at my vanity deflated my puffed-up ego. Their examples of humility and honesty both shamed and encouraged me. I was introduced to my muddy self by my muddied monastic family.

I notice several mammoth trucks lined up along the curb on University Avenue, waiting their turn to drive down the ramp. Muddy tires are leaving telltale tracks for blocks around.

Benedict is, as we might expect, into mud in a big way. The monastic life is intended to help us first to get in touch with the deepest truth of who we are, and then to help us use that truth to get closer to God. Besides giving humility its own long chapter, the Rule stresses several times the importance of recognizing your own mistakes and imperfections. Benedict prescribes punishments that will help the straying brother to "see the error of his ways." Part of the abbot's job is to help the monks admit their own shortcomings, and the Rule sets a very clear priority on facing one's imperfections squarely:

"Should anyone make a mistake in a psalm, responsory, refrain or reading, he must make satisfaction there before all. If he does not use this occasion to humble himself, he will be subjected to a more severe punishment for failing to correct by humility the wrong committed through negligence" (Rule, Chapter 45).

Every day I'm reminded of my human frailty and imperfection. In these moments of grace when I'm forced to look at myself, I'm faced with a crucial choice: I can either be humbled and led to intimacy with my brothers and with the God of truth, or I can turn away angrily and live a lie. This is why in Chapter 27 Benedict calls for wise seniors to be sent to a wavering brother to console and encourage him, so that he won't run away from the struggle with his own imperfections.

I continue my way down Branford Place with a renewed respect for the value of mud. You don't see much of it around downtown, but there's plenty of it at Newark Abbey. It is, after all, one of God's favorite things.

For Reflection

1. Saint Athanasius says that the Scriptures are a perfect mirror for us humans, in which we can each see our own faults and strengths reflected. Select a Scripture passage such as the incident with the rich young man (Mark 10:17–22), or the woman at the well (John 4:1–30). Then ask the Lord to let you see yourself in the mirror as you read. Do you recognize your reflection? If so, how does it make you feel? Uncomfortable? Ashamed? Is it a positive experience or a negative one?

2. What is God's favorite way of reminding you of your mud? When or where are you most aware of your own imperfections? Is there one person, place, or situation in particular that forces you to look at your mud?

3. Do you know someone who seems quite at home with his or her limitations? What do you think allows him or her to handle them so well? Is there something you could learn from this person?

4. Make up a prayer or a poem concerning your mud.

7
Sunday

The Sumac

A Theology of Messiness

The chain-link fence got there first. By the time the sumac tree started growing beside it, the fence was simply a given, like the ocean or the Alps. The fence made it impossible for the sapling to grow into a normal sumac with branches arranged neatly along a perfectly straight trunk.

The tree started to grow as best it could, though, accepting the soccer field fence as a fact of life. It poked its branches through the diamond-shaped holes and wrapped itself around the heavy wires until they became part of its very self. In the process its trunk, as thick as my wrist, got twisted and gnarled.

Since the William Street hill seems steep this afternoon, I've stopped on the way up to say hello to this homely sumac flopping its misshapen greenish-tan branches out over the sidewalk. As I look at all its peculiar twists and knots, it occurs to me that this tree is a living lesson about a deep spiritual reality: true happiness doesn't come from being perfect.

Mastery demands flawless performance—a computer program or an airplane engine that runs only most of the time isn't acceptable to anyone. Yet human beings are not called by Christ to that kind of perfection in the sense of flawlessness. We are called to be saints. Saints, though, aren't people who are without sin, but rather those who keep struggling to close the gap between the messiness of their actual situation and the glory of what they could be.

A spark plug works only when there's a gap between its two elements. An electrical charge is sent to the spark plug, creating a spark in that gap, which in turn explodes the gasoline in the cylinder and powers the engine. All the action is in the gap. A saint's life is similar: holiness is like the spark that happens in the gap between the actual and the ideal, in the realm of striving, struggling, and thirsting for God. Without that distance to be overcome, there can be no holiness.

By this definition, a perfect saint is a contradiction in terms, since someone who has arrived at perfection is no longer hungry for God, no longer struggling or striving or risking everything with the Lord.

We sometimes read about saints who achieved mastery over the forces of evil in their lives through heroic self-denial and asceticism. But this emphasis on mastery mustn't mislead us: it's not their mastery over anything, whether their body, their emotions, or some set of requirements, that makes them saints. Their holiness comes from their extraordinary intimacy with God: a deep, intense friendship with the Divine Lover. Holiness means being madly in love with a God who is madly in love with you.

The misshapen branches wave in the light breeze. For a moment it's as if the tree is nodding its thanks for my visit.

While a mastery approach wants to calculate and keep score, and will settle for nothing less than flawless competency, true intimacy knows that human imperfection (my own and others) is an inevitable part of any love relationship. St. Paul in his hymn to love in First Corinthians says, "Love is patient...it bears all things" (1 Corinthians 13:4,7). If holiness is about love, then it has to make a lot of allowance for mistakes, and has much more to do with imperfection that it does with flawlessness.

It takes some of us a while to make friends with our limitations. We spend years wishing that things were different: "If only I had a calmer disposition," "If only my parents hadn't gotten divorced," "If only my health were better." The person that God is inviting to intimacy, though, is not the ideal person I wish I were, but this person that I actually am, imperfect and flawed. Like the sumac tree limited by the fence, I've been shaped by my family upbringing, my genetic makeup, my cultural background, and so forth.

I nod good-bye to my tree friend and climb the last steep part of the hill alongside the abbey church, squinting up at the red brick bell tower. With a relaxing, raspy whisper the summer breeze is rattling the leaves of the maples that line the sidewalk.

The Rule expects that the community will contain a wide variety of characters, including some pretty weak ones who hide things in their mattresses, refuse correction, or strike others in anger. Benedict starts Chapter 27, on "The Abbot's Concern for the Excommunicated" this way: "[The abbot] must exercise the utmost care and concern for the wayward brothers, because it is not the healthy who need a physician, but the sick." A few verses later he writes, in a succinct contrast of intimacy and mastery, "He should realize that he has undertaken care of the sick, not tyranny over the healthy." The chapter on "The Daily Manual Labor" cautions that "all things are to be done with moderation on account of the fainthearted" and "On Sunday all are to be engaged in reading except those who have been assigned to various duties. If anyone is so remiss and indolent that he is unwilling or unable to study or to read, he is to be given some work in order that he may not be idle" (Rule, Chapter 48).

Benedict accepts such human weaknesses, and with uncanny shrewdness weaves them into the very fabric of the monastic life, the way the tree wisely embraces the inevitable wires of the fence. My little misshapen tree down the street takes the same approach to life as Benedict: the spirituality of messiness. Unlike the mastery mindset that refuses to accept imperfection, the spirituality of messiness says yes to my brokenness and my need for redemption. In the same breath, though, it also insists that I am loved unconditionally by an all-merciful Savior. It even invites me to value my imperfections as the way for God to get past my defenses and teach me humility and show me infinite forgiveness.

A tall, robust sumac lifts its branches above the high red-brick wall of the churchyard that borders the steep sidewalk. I notice how nicely the leaves are arranged.

The spirituality of messiness allows for the pleasant possibility that a particular fault or weakness of mine is not a problem to be mastered but a mystery to be lived. My struggle with impatience, for example, is certainly an important part of God's plan for me. Maybe it's my special share of Christ's suffering, or some mysterious way of calling me to divine intimacy.

Up at the corner of King Boulevard now, I turn right and pass in front of the abbey church, toward the front door of the monastery.

One of the happiest effects of the theology of messiness is that it changes the way we experience life in community. Once we come to accept the fact that we're imperfect, we suddenly find it easier to put up with the messiness of the people around us. Our faults give us community members a chance to practice patience and loving support of one another, the way Paul advises: "Help carry one another's' burdens; in that way you will fulfill the law of Christ" (Galatians 6:2). We can start to see the ordinary flaws of our brother monks and the mistakes of our students as reflections of our own familiar faults and struggles. As we learn to forgive ourselves for being imperfect, we learn to forgive them, too. Our messiness is, after all, our road to intimacy not only with Christ but also with our brothers and sisters.

As I dig out my key I check my wristwatch. Good! Still enough time for a little spiritual reading before all us sinners gather around the altar for community Eucharist.

For Reflection

1. In Matthew 9:9–13 Jesus tells the Pharisees, "Those who are well do not need a physician, but the sick do…I came to save not the self-righteous but sinners." What is there about yourself that you might present to the Divine Physician for healing? Can you bring to him the worst thing about you? Do you believe that God loves you no matter what?

2. What are some of the givens that shape your life? Think of one weakness or imperfection that you have trouble accepting or that you are resentful about. The theology of messiness would predict that this bad thing will in fact provide you with a special way to intimacy with God. You might read 2 Corinthians 11:30–12:10, where Paul reflects on the role of weakness and suffering in his relationship with Christ: "Therefore I am content with weakness…for when I am weak, then I am strong."

8
Monday

Clinton Place

A Theology of Busyness

She looks harried, as if she has too many things to do and too little time. That's probably why I notice the nicely dressed woman in her thirties marching purposefully with the crowd that's charging up Raymond Boulevard from the train station.

I glance into the front window of Starbucks at a young man in a rumpled suit coat hunched over his laptop typing feverishly, his cup of morning coffee forgotten beside him.

Our modern culture seems to force most of us into hectic busyness—we get pulled in ten directions at the same time by obligations to family, work, housekeeping, elderly parents, and so on. Our priorities get all jumbled as the practical demands of everyday reality leave us no time to devote to the truly important things such as deepening our relationship with husband or wife, spending time with close friends—or tending to the spiritual dimension of our life.

The dim reflections of dozens of commuters stream across the window glass in an endless, bustling parade.

It seems that these days earning a living, running a household, and making car payments are considered the real and important occupations of life. A person's relationship with God is an optional extra, on the same level as, say, a passion for model railroading. In the gospel vision of life, though, it's just the other way around: our eternal destiny and intimacy with God are the larger reality, the framework and context in which we live our everyday practical existence. All our work, play, joy, and suffering mean nothing except as they relate to the unseen realm of the spirit, and are seen as part of God's loving plan for us. This spiritual view of reality is crucial for Christians who are kept inhumanly busy by dozens of commitments.

How can we ever hope to stay focused on the spiritual dimension of reality during a hectic work day? Surprisingly, some time-tested and very practical helps for lay people can be found in the Christian monastic tradition.

For instance, many people would swear that they spend hours at work every day without seeing any reminders of God's presence. Benedict, however, tells them to look again. We meet Jesus all the time, he insists, in every single person we encounter. The incarnation wasn't just some event that lasted 33 years some 2,000 years ago. Jesus continues to take flesh every day in all the people around us.

Chapter 53 of the Rule, "On the Reception of Guests," says, "Great care and concern are to be shown in receiving poor people and pilgrims, because in them more particularly Christ is received." Chapter 36, "On the Care of Sick Brothers," begins, "Care of the sick must rank above and before all else, so that they may be truly served as Christ." Dealing with other people is one sure way of meeting the living God I'm seeking.

Benedict cautions that sometimes it's the suffering Christ that comes into my life, waiting at the monastery door for a sandwich, or acting up in religion class, or being unreasonable in the office. That's when it's hardest—and most important—to remember that Christ is in everyone. If I develop the habit of automatically seeing Christ in all of the people around me, then I've found a way to stay aware, stay focused on the one thing necessary even in the midst of the busiest and most stressful day.

As I reach Clinton Place a knot of pedestrians charges around the corner, forcing me to stop short. I peek carefully around the end of Starbucks before stepping to the curb to wait for the light to change.

A second help toward a spirituality of busyness comes from Benedict's emphasis on interior disposition. He insists, for example, that outward obedience doesn't count if I obey with an ill will or grudgingly. In another place he encourages his followers, "Let us stand to sing the psalms in such a way that our minds are in harmony with our voices." The idea is that everything ultimately depends on my attitude and motivation. If I treat all my daily tasks (including housekeeping, parenting, and earning a salary) simply as challenges for me to master and control, then they easily become a source of tremendous stress. Everything changes, however, once I consider my busyness as a major way of loving my family, my way of using my God-given talents for building up the kingdom. I used to feel frazzled and pressured by the constant deadlines when doing our school's computerized scheduling and grades reporting. Then all of a sudden one day my responsibilities seemed much less of a burden to me: I had started to look at that job as my special way of loving 500 students. The pressure and the stress were still there, but no longer as the grim price exacted by my attempts at mastery. They had become simply an inconvenience that went along with my unique way of serving the kids.

A handsome young man in a three-piece suit is waving at me from across the street. I recognize him as he dodges a couple of cars to come over and say hello.

"Tarik! How are you! It's been a long time!"

"Father Al! How you been! You look the same as when I had you for French!"

"You're not looking so bad yourself. What are you up to these days?"

"Well, I've started my own computer consulting firm." He proudly produces his business card and hands it to me. "It's been going for almost two years, and we're doing okay." As I read his name on the little card I can't hide my pleasure at seeing how well he's done. (Whatever his work is, I know it can't require knowing any French!) After a little small talk and a promise to stop by school soon, he disappears quickly into the crowd, in a hurry to get to some appointment.

Four young women wearing white socks and sneakers with their business outfits stride up to the corner shoulder to shoulder, chatting happily with one another.

All the famous saints speak of God as their intimate friend. But intimacy makes demands on us. For example, a close personal relationship—whether with a spouse or with God—needs to be nurtured by a certain amount of undistracted, deep conversation. Even if you can't spend long hours at prayer you still have to spend at least some quiet time devoted specifically to it. But what if your life is so busy that there's no time for it? Interestingly, magazine articles are always offering busy people advice on how to find time in their schedules for things they really want to do. So look again—maybe there really is a way for you to make the time.

Many busy Christians probably have a more intimate relationship with God than they realize, thanks to a constant inner dialogue: "Thank you, Jesus!" "Lord, please give me patience!" "Dear God, show me how I'm supposed to get all this stuff done by eleven o'clock!" Through such brief moments of conversation they hang out with God all day long. Spending a lot of time just sharing everyday tasks and conversation is, of course, a well-known way of building intimacy with someone. So, keeping up a running conversation with the Lord is another step toward having a lively relationship with God, even in the midst of the busiest day.

These little ways of cultivating intimacy with the Divine can whet my appetite for a deeper relationship. Once I get drawn deeper and deeper into the divine heart, who knows where the Lord may choose to lead me then?

As the commuters pour into 744 Broad, where my father had his law office for so many years, I picture God smiling with delight, busily fashioning a unique, personal, special relationship with each one of these busy folks—including me!

For Reflection

1. When you read Luke 10:38–42, the story of Jesus' visit with Martha and Mary, who do you identify with first, Martha the active doer, or Mary the quiet listener? Saint Gregory the Great says that Martha and Mary are sisters who have to learn to live together in harmony under the same roof. The problem comes when Martha loses her sense of perspective. In verse 41, Jesus says, "Martha, Martha, you worry and fret about so many things, and yet few are needed. Indeed, only one." Imagine the Lord saying that to you today. What particular things is he referring to in your life that cause you to "worry and fret?" Did you choose them? What is your attitude toward each of them? Can you shorten the list of things you fret about? Has your Martha ever completely taken over your life with her relentless busyness, keeping you so preoccupied with everyday concerns that you lost sight of what was really important?

2. Think of one particularly stressful task or activity in your present life. Now assume that it is actually a call to get closer to God, and ask the Lord to help you to see how this is supposed to help you grow in love. Maybe it allows you to meet Christ by putting you in contact with other people, or gives you an opportunity to serve others. Or perhaps it's simply your small but unavoidable share in Christ's suffering right now.

3. If you already converse with God during the day, what kinds of things do you talk about? Do you treat God as a friend? A fixer? A complaint department? How might you make better use of your chats with the Lord?

9

Sidewalk Rage

Trusting Your Emotions

As the light turns green I take a deep breath of fresh spring air and stride onto the crosswalk. I glance carefully over my right shoulder checking for any cars turning left off of Rodgers Boulevard, then continue may way across Bergen Street in Harrison. This is the halfway point on my seventy-minute afternoon walk.

The blast of a car's horn and the squeal of speeding tires just inches behind me send me scrambling for my life. Convinced that I'm about to be run over, I dive the final few feet to the opposite curb. I reach the sidewalk, and I wheel around to see a bright red car with four teenagers in it escaping down the side street.

My heart is still pounding as I stop to gather my wits. Idiots! They probably thought the whole thing was pretty funny! They could have killed me! Don't they have any sense at all? You could give somebody a heart attack doing that! My face is hot with indignation. Besides, they're cowards. Took off so they didn't have to face me! I realize that I'm just getting myself all worked up for nothing, so I turn to continue my walk, trying not to let my sidewalk rage spoil an otherwise beautiful day.

I start to think about this whole strange business of anger. Co-workers physically assaulting one another on the job. Frustrated mothers beating their infants unconscious. Bizarre cases of road rage and airport rage appearing on news broadcasts. Irate fathers attacking Little League umpires. It's no wonder that angry has come to mean ugly, destructive and violent. Of all the emotions, anger seems to be, at least in our culture, one of the most problematic. Misunderstanding it causes a lot of needless guilt and worry. You hear people say "A Christian isn't supposed to get angry at anyone," or "I got furious at my four-year-old for writing all over the new wallpaper with a Magic Marker; then I felt guilty and had to go to Confession," or "I know I shouldn't feel angry, even against the person who abused me when I was seven years old." We're taught early on that certain emotions are acceptable and others aren't, so we think that some emotions must be morally okay and others evil. We learn that anger is always wrong, which in turn causes us to feel ashamed when we get angry. Then, since we're ashamed of our anger, we deny it and stuff it somewhere inside instead of dealing honestly with it. Finally, because we haven't dealt honestly with it, the bottled-up emotion eventually bursts out, but by now it's grown into fury—forceful, unexpected, ugly, and even destructive—which seems to prove the original point that anger is a bad thing.

On the concrete wall of the overpass for Route 280 I notice some graffiti spray-painted in an irritated scrawl that I can't quite decipher. Which is probably just as well.

Like any other emotion, though, anger in itself is neither good nor bad. Emotions pop up uninvited and aren't something that we choose, so they can't be morally right or wrong in themselves. Personal moral responsibility has to involve making a free choice, so the sudden urge, say, to punch my boss in the nose can't be right or wrong. It's only when I decide what to do about this feeling that the issue of good or evil comes up.

It's true that an angry disposition, anger as a permanent way of life, is a vice—fruitless and death-dealing. Thinkers in every time and culture agree that anger accounts for a large portion of the world's unhappiness. Anger doesn't have to be destructive or ugly, however. In fact, it often proves very useful, moving people to found orphanages, launch campaigns against drunk driving, and perform deeds of heroism.

The fact is that the mastery approach to life mistrusts all emotions because they're unpredictable and irrational, and it tries to avoid or suppress them whenever possible. Intimacy, on the other hand, can't exist without them.

That's because intimacy means sharing who I am, and my emotions are an essential part of me. So, letting someone know how I feel is a great way of sharing my true self. Of course, it means leaving myself vulnerable—when I give you a glimpse of my deepest self, and share even my darkest feelings, I'm trusting that you won't throw your hands up in horror and run away forever. Healthy human relationships have to involve emotions.

A car cruises by pulsing with the thudding bass of a loud rap song. Its open windows let everyone hear the irate voice of the singer shouting something about not caring.

The refusal to feel our own anger has repercussions in the spiritual life, too. It stands to reason that if being angry at other humans is bad, then being angry at God is absolutely taboo. The very thought sends chills up pious Christian spines. "I know it's a sin to get mad at God, so I just don't say anything." "I'm afraid he'll strike me with lightning!"

But the principles of healthy intimacy are still at work in the spiritual life. Even between an individual and God, accepting the other means accepting that person's feelings as well. If true intimacy demands that I honestly share my emotions with the other, then sharing my emotions with God is an essential part of my spiritual life.

The scene of our Lady of Fatima and the three little children glistens blue and white on four hand-painted enamel tiles set into the brick front of a new house.

My ability to be emotional with God depends on my image of what God is like. If the Deity is some aloof, short-tempered, vengeful, power-tripping old crank, then it makes sense to avoid showing even the slightest impatience or displeasure—let alone anger! This is a mastery-based relationship, where power and self-protection are the driving forces.

The God revealed by Jesus, however, is someone who loves me infinitely, who delights in my every action, who suffers when I suffer, and is constantly inviting me to intimacy. There's nothing—absolutely nothing—that I can say or do or feel that will make this God stop loving me. I experienced this when my brother died of cancer some years ago. During a long and painful grieving process I was so angry at God for awhile that I told people "God and I aren't speaking." By the time this rocky period of hurt and anger was over, though, I actually felt a lot closer to the Lord, who had been my compassionate and faithful friend and had stayed around and put up with my childish ranting. How freeing it is when you finally find out that being angry can actually be okay!

I come to a quiet intersection. Before I set foot in the crosswalk this time, though, I take an extra-careful look over my right shoulder watching for sneaky teenage drivers making sudden left turns.

For Reflection

1. We read in Ephesians 4:26, "Do not let the sun go down on your anger." Are you able to let someone know in a constructive way when you are angry with them? If this is difficult for you, you might pray to the Lord for help with it.

2. Several psalms in the Bible are complaints, even angry ones, against a God who seems absent: "My God, my God, why have you forsaken me?" "Why do you no longer march forth with our armies?" Have you ever felt angry or disappointed with God? What was that experience like? Did you feel sad? Hurt? Angry? Did you tell God how you felt? How did it affect your relationship with the Lord?

10

The Street Fair

Glimpses of Glory

Lemon yellow, hot pink, Day-Glo green. The polo shirts on the sidewalk racks are partying in the warm spring sunlight. The lazy breeze, drenched in the oily aroma of sausage and peppers, pulses with a bright salsa beat blaring from a boombox. This first day of real summer-like weather has drawn crowds of winter-weary Newarkers to Broad and Market for an impromptu Saturday afternoon street fair.

I have to slow down and thread my way carefully through the cheerful crush on Market Street. But I don't mind: I'm thoroughly enjoying the sunshine and warm air—and the sleeveless blouses, tube tops, and feminine curves that have been hidden for months under heavy winter clothes.

"Father Al!"

One of my students is standing in front of me accompanied by two teenage girls.

"Hey, Robert! How are you! Some weather, huh? You down here shopping?"

"No. Mostly just chillin'."

"And who are these two good-looking people?" The girls giggle self-consciously.

"Oh! Sorry! Ummm...Father Albert, this is Tyisha. And this is Rhonda."

"Nice to meet you." I say. "Isn't this a great day to be outside!"

"Yup!" agrees Robert. "We just got off the bus. Well, guess we're gonna walk around for a while."

I take the hint: "So, listen, don't let me hold you up. Ladies, it was nice meeting you. Robert, take care."

"Okay. See you Monday!" he answers. Rhonda gives a big smile. Tyisha waves a bashful good-bye.

As I watch them cross the street I think to myself, "Now those are two pretty girls!" In fact, maybe it's just my lively imagination, but on this pleasant April afternoon all the girls are starting to look extra-pretty.

Some people think that if you have a vow of celibacy you're not supposed to notice certain kinds of beauty in God's creation. They figure that as a celibate you renounce your sexuality—as if a human could just give up being a sexual creature. They think that you climb inside this sacred glass bottle and isolate yourself from any kind of close human interaction. You deny any sexual attractions, stifle your emotions, and avoid all close personal relationships, especially with people of the opposite sex. But that sort of celibacy is mastery at its worst: it's exactly the opposite of what Christ is really calling us to.

Human beings are created in the image of God, a God who is love. In other words, we're made for love, it's what gives our life meaning. All Christians have the same vocation: to imitate Jesus, the Man for Others, through a life of self-giving love. Christ (who was celibate, remember!) taught us by his example how to be fully human. He lived for others, listening, consoling, touching, and healing, until finally, in the ultimate act of intimacy, he laid down his life for us.

As a monk and a celibate, I'm called to live in a whole web of human relationships, all of them rooted in love: my brothers in the monastery, my family, my close friends, both men and women, my students, and so on. It's in this climate of love that I find the meaning of my solitude and of my celibacy.

A bride in her wedding gown and a groom in his black tux smile from a large color photo in a store window. They're peering intently into the camera as if it were a crystal ball and they were looking for a glimpse of their future together.

Pope John Paul II writes somewhere that marriage is the human experience that begins to make God comprehensible to human beings because it is a reflection of the inner life of the Trinity, the ideal example of mutual self-giving. To the eyes of faith, marriage is an outward, sacramental sign of the union between God and us.

To those same eyes of faith, celibate life, too, is a sacramental sign. It points to another fundamental spiritual truth: the fact that every human person is incurably incomplete. Although all of the earthly loves we experience are part of one divine, infinite Love, they are all bounded by time and space and human limitations. No matter how wonderful and deep the love we may share with another, human intimacy alone can't satisfy us completely because the intimacy we're created for is intimacy with the Infinite. Anything less is destined to leave us disappointed and unfulfilled. "Ultimately" as Ronald Rolheiser so poignantly puts it, "we all sleep alone." It's simply a fact of the human condition, no matter how close we get to someone.

A teenager with beautiful jet-black hair framing her striking Latino features strolls past holding hands with a handsome young man in a red two-strap undershirt. They're each listening to their own separate Walkman players.

My celibate vocation lived joyfully and generously ought to remind others that there's always more. It should point to a kingdom that lies beyond this world, and to a day when all our incompleteness will be overcome and all our longings will be satisfied by God alone.

The street fair gives way to a quiet calm as I walk north along Broad Street. I stop at a corner. Then, as the light turns green, a high-school age girl tugging her five-year-old brother comes toward me. Her face is so pretty I feel a catch in my throat, a bittersweet tug, a familiar ache deep inside. Another little inkling of my incurable incompleteness, a reminder that my soul and body will both be restless until they rest in God.

Each of us, celibate, married, single or widowed, is constantly catching glimpses of the Divine. They're all around us: a loving relationship, a generous act of kindness, a gorgeous sunset, or the beauty of a young girl's face.

A short, silent man with the chiseled features of an Inca sits impassively beside a cart that is bulging with beautiful flowers. I'm dazzled by the bouquets of crimson carnations sprinkled with sprigs of baby's breath and wrapped in clear cellophane cones. Bundles of slender gladioli the color of lemons and apricots nod gently in the breeze. Armfuls of tulips glowing yellow, white, red, and pink burst from shiny tin pots. The whole little wagon is an exuberant celebration of God's beauty, a perfect parable of spring.

A prayer starts to rise in my heart. Thank you, Lord of Love, for this glorious afternoon. For the bright blue sky, and the gentle, sleepy breeze. For the street fair and the gorgeous colors of the flowers. For the pretty faces and feminine figures. Thanks for all these sparkling splinters of your infinite splendor, these previews of heaven's loveliness. Thanks for keeping me hungry for you, and for calling me to celebrate my unfinishedness in a life of joyful celibate love.

Raymond Boulevard. A turn to the left will take me back to the monastery in less than ten minutes. I check my watch. Two-thirty.

Turning right, I head across Broad Street. Still plenty of time for a few more glimpses of God's glory.

For Reflection

1. Many passages from the Old Testament reflect our longing for completeness: "My soul yearns for you in the night, yes, my spirit within me keeps vigil for you" (Isaiah 26:9). "My soul is thirsting for the living God" (Psalms 42:3). "O God, you are my God who I seek; for you my flesh pines and my soul thirsts" (Psalms 63:2). "My heart and my flesh cry out for the living God" (Psalms 84:3). What are some of the ways that this longing and yearning show up in your own life? How do you respond to the feeling? How do you think others may have been affected by your response?

2. Take a few minutes to imagine how your life might change if you were to respond fully to the call to divine intimacy. Ask the Lord to help you answer the invitation more generously.

3. As a celibate I sometimes feel a certain emptiness, an ache of incompleteness deep inside. It may happen, for instance, when I'm visiting a family as little children are being given baths and being put to bed. Do you ever experience that hollowness, that haunting sense of incompleteness? If so, where? What is your response to it? Do you deny it? Resist it? Ignore it? What do you think God may want you to do with that feeling?

4. Make up a prayer about your incompleteness.

PART THREE

Stay Vulnerable

11
———

Juan

You Know Not the Day

Angry gray smoke billows up from the Manhattan skyline thirteen miles to the east, and stretches southward across the September sky like a tattered funeral pall. I lean on the rail of Newark's Jackson Street Bridge to stare at the ugly cloud boiling up from the spot where the World Trade Towers stood just twenty-four hours ago. My elbows, resting on the railing, pick up the earthquake vibrations of the traffic rumbling behind me.

Yesterday's assaults on New York and Washington marked the end of something. Americans used to feel immune from terrorist attacks, but now we see that there are people in the world, maybe even in our own neighborhoods, who are bent on destroying us as individuals and as a nation. As I stare at the trail of oily smoke, a heavy, overwhelming sadness starts to weigh me down.

The loud honk of a truck's horn jerks me back into today. I turn away from the ugly, eloquent cloud and continue plodding across toward Market Street, the concrete sidewalk of the bridge shuddering under my feet. The traffic seems to be hurrying along as usual. On second thought, maybe there's an undertone of dark uneasiness beneath the noisy bustle?

The president has put our armed forces on a state of highest alert. We're suddenly vigilant, in a suspicious mindset that will make us frisk airline passengers and scan whole buildings for suspected biological weapons. We've now become a nation preoccupied with security.

Vigilance is a Christian virtue that monastics have always lived out in a special way. At the beginning of the Prologue to the Rule, Benedict quotes Paul: "It is high time for us to rise from sleep," to open our ears and listen for the divine voice that calls us each day. The monastic practice of getting up in the very early hours of the morning to pray vigils is a dramatic sign of watching for the Bridegroom who, Scripture warns us, will return in the middle of the night, at an hour when we least expect him. That's what happened to poor Juan. I've been thinking about him since last night.

Five of us priests from the abbey are taken on a whirlwind ride in the back of a sheriff's department van to Port Authority police headquarters at the New Jersey end of the Holland Tunnel, just across the river from the World Trade Center. There is an unnatural hush inside the almost empty office building where we are going to make phone calls to families of dozens of missing Port Authority police officers.

At last we're escorted upstairs, where a haggard captain hands us computer-printed personnel sheets. They each show a color I.D. photo, a name, an address, and a phone number of a missing officer. As he hands me my stack he taps the top sheet. "This guy here, his wife is due to have a baby any day now. Just so you know." I sit in someone's work cubicle and stare down at the phone. Next to it is a framed photo of a young family—a little blond girl in a blue dress sitting between her beaming parents. To my right, tacked to the cubicle wall, is a small poster with the poem "Footprints" printed on a seascape. I scrawl four phrases on a yellow legal pad so I won't forget what to say when someone answers the phone: "N_____ is still missing and unaccounted for." "Do you have someone with you now?" "Is there anything we can do for you?" "We'll contact you as soon as we know anything definite." I make the Sign of the Cross and pick up the phone.

The first two calls are heart-wrenching even though the spouses are too deep in shock to show any emotion. Then I come to my third sheet. The slightly-blurred color photograph of a good-looking young officer (I'll call him Juan) smiles up at me from the page as I dial his home phone. It rings once, twice, three times. At the fourth ring a cheerful recorded voice clicks on, "Hi! This is Juan! I'm not here right now. Just leave your number and I'll get back to you right away." The machine beeps. Staring down at his young face, I put the receiver back reverently, with the eerie feeling that I've just heard a dead man talking to me on the phone.

Juan had no idea when he left for work in the morning that his plans, his dreams, and his life were all about to end suddenly and violently. I keep thinking about him and praying for him.

Up ahead I see the train station with its Amtrak lines that follow the eastern seaboard from Florida to Boston. There are police cars blocking the street behind the station where the buses used to stop, and uniformed officers are standing uneasily at barricades to keep vehicles from getting too close.

The Rule encourages us to moral watchfulness:

"Live in fear of judgment day and have a great horror of hell. Yearn for everlasting life with holy desire. Day by day remind yourself that you are going to die. Hour by hour keep careful watch over all you do…. As soon as wrongful thoughts come into your heart, dash them against Christ and disclose them to your spiritual father" (Rule, 4:44–50).

Despite the talk of fear of hell, Benedict emphasizes that the reason for our vigilance is the holy desire for heaven. The cure for wrongful thoughts has nothing to do with mastery, but involves acts of intimacy: drawing closer to Christ and opening your heart to a spiritual father.

I walk in front of the barricades and follow the sidewalk along Market Street where it passes underneath the station.

There are so-called religious people who go through their entire lives in a state of highest alert. They see just about everything as a threat to their salvation. The tiniest distraction during prayer, for example, is an incursion of the devil and must be fought off with every weapon available. The slightest stirring of sexual feeling is a terrorist plot calling for immediate and harsh countermeasures. Life is for them an unrelenting, joyless project of fending off the devil's attacks. Everyone, including friends, family, and maybe even God, is a potential threat to their personal mastery project of saving their own soul.

This kind of grim super-control is not pious watchfulness but an obsession with keeping absolute command of life, a self-centered grasping for mastery. It's the opposite of vigilance. Although vigilance certainly requires sacrifice and constant watchfulness, its goal is not mastery but intimacy. We are on a journey from fear to love, from slavery to freedom:

"Now, therefore, after ascending all these steps of humility, the monk will quickly arrive at that perfect love of God which casts out fear. Through this love, all that he once performed with dread, he will now begin to observe without effort, as though naturally, from habit, no longer out of fear of hell, but out of love for Christ, good habit and delight in virtue. All this the Lord will, by the Holy Spirit graciously manifest in his workman now cleansed of vices and sins" (Rule, 7:67-70).

The monastic version of highest alert, then, is not nervous jumpiness in the face of danger, but rather serene mindfulness—a measure of just how much we value our relationship with God. It is the ongoing, patient process of keeping ourselves free of clutter and excess baggage as we go on our joyful journey toward God's tent. It keeps us ready to welcome the Lord at any time.

Emerging on the other side of the station, I see that there are only a couple of ambulances still parked in front. The rest of the scene looks like any other afternoon: trucks and delivery vans jostle each other along Market Street. Shoppers and commuters crowd the sidewalk near the corner of Broad. You'd hardly guess that we're on highest alert. A young couple holding hands whisper to one other as they stroll in the autumn sunshine.

I wonder if Juan had a girlfriend.

For Reflection

1. Read Matthew 25:1–13, the parable of the wise and the foolish virgins. Is there some particular area of behavior or some attitude in which you have grown drowsy lately, making intimacy with God difficult?

2. What particular weaknesses of yours are likely to show up when you let down your vigilance?

12

Shadow People

Living in the Light

Leaning over the banister, I glance down at the dark sidewalk under the Jackson Street bridge. Just the usual collection of empty wine bottles and fast food containers, an old sofa and a few scraps of carpet. This is a corner of the mysterious world of the shadow people. I call them that because I hardly ever lay eyes on them. I just see the traces they leave all over the city: a cardboard refrigerator-carton shelter under the steps where Raymond Boulevard passes under King, or the food scraps and filthy rags scattered in the grimy darkness along Edison Place where it cuts under Penn Station.

Now and then I pass a shadow person lying hidden under some sheets of newspaper along the sidewalk somewhere, and wonder what it must feel like to have no one who knows you or cares about you, no one who consoles you or challenges you, no one you can count on. You're on your own, all alone in a shadow world, hidden from everyone else's gaze, and disconnected from the rest of humanity.

In the Book of Genesis God decides that it is not good for Adam to be alone. A few verses later Adam is sharing the joys of the garden with Eve, and both are chatting easily and openly with God. Paradise is a delight for all three of them because of their connectedness and closeness.

Human beings are, after all, made in the image of a God who is Love itself:

a trinity of divine persons united in eternal, joyful mutual self-giving. Relatedness is at the core of who we are. It's not good for us to be alone.

I'm halfway across the bridge. To my right is the gray cardboard cutout of the Manhattan skyline. Off to my left, down on the river, a small aluminum skiff skims downstream with a single, lonesome figure slouched at the outboard motor in the stern.

It occurs to me that the homeless aren't the only shadow people around. There are a lot of folks who live alone and hidden right in the midst of their marriage, their family, their neighbors, or their religious community. They avoid the risk of close relationships by not letting anyone get near enough to really know them. Fearful and lonely, these people, too, live in their own little shadow world.

Christian life, and in fact any authentically human life, is a life of connectedness, of vulnerability and self-giving. Paul tells us that our existence gets its very meaning from our being all joined as members of one body.

A Harrison Police car gliding in the opposite direction beeps at me, and the officer at the wheel waves. I wave back before I realize who it is. He graduated about fifteen years ago from the school where I teach. Good guy. Bet he's a really good cop.

The whole purpose of the Christian life is to seek union with God—not a God who lives in solitary splendor, but one who is a dynamic loving relationship of three Persons. Benedict envisions this search happening with the help of a loving community whose members work constantly at staying connected with one another, with their superior, and with God. Everything about the monastery encourages connectedness, starting with the sharing of the same schedule, communal prayer, and a common table. The vows of obedience and the common ownership of goods build community and help us develop a sense of depending on God and others. Even celibacy

invites the monastic out of the self-centered shadows into a life of cheerful, generous, healthy human relationships.

I stride under the railroad bridge that passes over Rodgers Boulevard in Harrison, and notice how cool it is in the shade. A few steps later I'm back out into the light once more, feeling the hot summer sun warming the back of my damp shirt.

Benedict builds into the monastic life a number of practices that help the members stay connected with the rest of the community. For one thing, a monk is to share with his abbot or a wise elder "all the movements of his heart," so as to keep himself living not in darkness but in the bright light of day. Sharing your feelings, moods, and experiences with someone else is still a profitable and life-giving thing for anyone.

You ask simple permissions of your superior not with the idea of remaining an immature child, but because presenting your wishes or intentions to another for scrutiny is an exercise in self-disclosure and humility as well as a way of staying connected with the community.

In Chapter 49, "The Observance of Lent," Benedict won't allow a member of the community to practice a lenten penance without first telling the Abbot about it, so that there won't be any private asceticism going on in the shadows.

When a brother is having a hard time, the normal response for most males, it seems, is to say, "He's having a hard time, so we'd better back off and give him some space. He can work it out by himself. If he needs our help, he'll ask." Benedict, however, knowing the human temptation to withdraw and disconnect in times of trouble, tells the abbot to send in "mature and wise brothers who, under the cloak of secrecy, may support the wavering brother...and console him lest he be overwhelmed by excessive sorrow..." (Rule, Chapter 27). No one should have to live in the shadows!

There are times when I'm tempted to hide in the shadow world. If I'm upset or angry it sometimes seems easier to withdraw from the rest of the community and carry my burden alone. That way I don't have to go into long explanations or try to get someone else to understand how I feel. I just keep it to myself.

When something a community member did to me is bothering me, it often seems easier to just keep the hurt stuffed inside instead of confronting the person in a truthful, loving way. Living alone in the shadows appears at first to be a lot safer. But by refusing to confront a problem that needs to be brought into the light of day I'm choosing a dangerous world of denial, secrecy, and fear. The times when I've had the courage to meet a brother in the daylight, both of us have come away better for it.

I turn down Bergen Street, and in a minute I've plunged into the shadows of the Route 280 overpass. The traffic on the low six-lane bridge rumbles overhead like ominous, threatening thunder.

Benedict says that I can't pray and at the same time try to hide from God in the shadows of a secret inner world. He assumes that when I show up for prayer I'm going to bring my emotions along. For him tears and compunction of heart are a normal part of the prayer experience. Yet sometimes I hold back, afraid to bring my full, passionate, emotional self to God in prayer. The Lord can't be interested in that stuff, I lie to myself. Why bother telling God, "I'm scared to death" or "I'm so depressed I want to cry"? Better to just stay on safe ground and avoid anything too risky or revealing. Then, still unconnected, I sit in the shadows and rattle off someone else's words that have little to do with me or God.

I step out from under the bridge and squint into the brightness ahead. Rows of neat brick houses line both sides of the street, their short driveways lined with red and yellow flowers. Purple petunias bloom in a bed on one of the tiny, tended lawns. Two women, deep in conversation, are standing on the sidewalk in a patch of sunlight.

For Reflection

1. In Paul's description of the mystical body, Christ is the head and we are the members. Where is this interconnectedness most evident in your own life?

2. Paul encourages us in Ephesians 5:8, "Let us live as children of the light." Have you ever found yourself hiding in the land of shadows? Was it a conscious decision on your part? How did you get out?

3. Has anyone ever done something that invited you to come out of the shadows and walk in the light? Are there some practical ways that you might do the same for someone you know?

4. Two of many additional texts about being children of the light are 1 Thessalonians 5:4–5 and Colossians 1:12–13.

13

Empty Sky

Tapestry Story

The traffic seems strangely subdued this afternoon. As I stand on the corner of Bridge Street by the baseball stadium waiting for the light to change, an ambulance hustles by, heading north on Route 21. It's from a town forty miles south of here. Any other day that would seem odd, but not today, September 11, 2001. There are lots of strange things going on today. The ambulance is almost certainly heading for New York to help with the rescue work.

The terrible, awesome scene from this morning's television news replays itself over and over in my head: the two World Trade Center towers collapsing into clouds of dust and smoke. It's beyond imagining: The two tallest buildings in Manhattan just crashing to the ground and vanishing in seconds!

Many thoughtful people had already been saying that our whole modern world is falling apart. Traditional cultural and moral values have given way to materialism and selfishness, while advances in areas such as genetic engineering and information technology are changing our lives much faster than we can ever hope to adjust or adapt. And now this morning's insanity.

A time of terror and turmoil. Everything falling apart. It sounds like the days of the barbarian invasions! When Saint Benedict was born in 480, bands of marauding Goths were looting their way up and down the Italian peninsula while the familiar world of imperial Rome fell to pieces. The social and political orders were crumbling and the economic system was collapsing into rubble. People lived under a dark cloud of foreboding and pessimism.

In the midst of this turmoil, young Benedict of Nursia was sent by his parents to study in a dying and decadent Rome; but he soon left in disgust to seek God in the hills as a hermit. Later on, using his experiences as a monk and an abbot, and drawing on two centuries of monastic literature, Benedict would set down a way of life for others who were also seeking intimacy with God.

I'm across Route 21 and starting onto the Bridge Street bridge. Some vague feeling is bothering me. I don't know exactly what it is, but something's odd.

Considering the chaos caused by the collapse of the imperial government, and the frequent attacks by marauding Goths, Benedict should have designed a spiritual citadel sealed up securely behind high stone walls, its inmates preoccupied with defending themselves and their faith from the terrifying threats of a crumbling world. He knew, however, that a lifestyle which is closed up, defensive, and fearful will never lead to an encounter with the Divine. He saw that his goal of passionate connectedness with God would require not a closed system of security and mastery, but a loving community devoted to a life of openness, risk-taking, and intimacy. So it was that in that era of unprecedented confusion and destruction was born an astonishing and enduring vision: a life of Christian community based on trust, openness, and optimism. This is the vision that Benedict set down in his Rule for Monks which we Benedictines still follow today.

I'm halfway across the bridge and still can't place what's wrong. It's getting a little unnerving.

What makes Benedict's remarkable accomplishment possible is this: he views everything from a scriptural perspective. In his monastery you take Sacred Scripture personally, and fully expect it to speak to you and challenge you. The Bible gives practical directions for your life (for example, the number of prayer times per day) and provides the motivation for the basic monastic practices such as hospitality. Even the vows of obedience and poverty are motivated by the conscious imitation of the Christ of the Gospels.

The daily routine steeps you in Scripture: you spend hours a day singing psalms and listening to biblical readings in the liturgy, you devote time to studying and memorizing the psalms, and you might even hear passages being read from the Bible while you eat.

Aha! That's it! Finally I've figured out what's wrong! I turn and put both hands on the cool steel railing of the bridge and carefully scan the wide sky over the river. Newark International Airport is a few miles straight ahead, and Laguardia and Kennedy are way off to the left. You can always spot a couple of jetliners somewhere over Newark. And that's what's so strange: the sky is empty! I haven't seen or heard a plane or a helicopter all day. The airports are shut down tight. Satisfied now, I turn and continue across the bridge, listening to the mournful, whining hum of tires on the steel grid of the roadway.

At the center of Benedict's biblical approach to living is the practice of *lectio divina*, in which you slowly and meditatively read a page of Scripture, waiting for a word or a phrase to speak to your heart about your own life situation. After a while you start to see your own story as part of the one vast ongoing saga of God's saving love for the world. The same God who wrestled with Jacob at the ford of the Jabbok (Genesis 32:25–31) and called to Moses from the burning bush (Exodus 3:4) comes into your life every day in the situations and people you encounter. Everything in your life has a sacred dimension because each daily situation is part of salvation history.

Being immersed in the scriptural atmosphere of the monastery can give you a certain serene perspective on life's problems and tragedies—even terrorist attacks. God's loving plan for us, you see, isn't always supposed to be nice. Certainly the divine design often reveals itself in the beauty of a child's smile or the warmth of a close friendship. But the Bible shows that God's plan sometimes works itself out through tragedies, weaknesses, and even sin: Joseph's brothers sell him into slavery, David arranges the death of Uriah out of murderous lust for Bathsheba, the Chosen People are dragged off to captivity in Babylon, and Judas betrays Jesus with a kiss.

At the heart of the story of God's love lies the mystery of suffering. It's part of the main plot of the history of salvation—and of my own story. The essential message of the Gospel is that nothing ends at the foot of the cross on Good Friday, but instead the story keeps right on going to Easter Sunday when defeat is transformed into victory, and death into eternal life. As hard as this may be to remember this afternoon, terror and death never, ever have the last word.

When I look at a beautiful tapestry on the wall of a European cathedral, I recognize right away the characters and events from some Bible story such as the raising of Lazarus. If I were to look at the reverse side of that tapestry, though, I'd probably see nothing but a chaotic mess of snarls and knots that makes no sense at all. There's no hint of the biblical tale that I see from the front. Faith tells me that the Lord sees the tapestry of human existence from the side with the picture on it, and from that angle everything makes sense. Meanwhile I usually get to see only the incomprehensible, ugly side. Living in a scriptural world and immersing myself in the ongoing story of salvation keeps me anchored in the belief that from God's side all of my story, even the tragic and painful parts, not only makes sense, but is in fact unspeakably beautiful.

A commuter train clatters across the nearby bridge, returning from Hoboken. At least the trains are running again.

For Reflection

1. Read one or more of these Scripture passages, or maybe choose one of your own. Try to see yourself in the story as you read it. Put yourself in the place of various characters in the narrative, not just one. How does this account relate to your own story past or present?

• slavery and oppression in Egypt (Exodus 5:6–21)

• liberation and victory at the Sea of Reeds (Exodus 13:17—14:31)

• wandering in the wilderness (Exodus 16, 17)

• Jesus' healing the cripple (Luke 5:17–26)

• the parable of the Good Samaritan (Luke 10:29–37)

2. Is there one scriptural event or story that seems to describe particularly well your own situation today?

14

Y2K

Surprise! Surprise!

The sidewalk of the Jackson Street Bridge shivers nervously under my feet as cars and delivery trucks rumble along beside me.

Newark's corporate towers stand out clear against the wintry sky, reflecting the early morning sun. It's probably just my imagination, but I sense that the office buildings lining the river are all holding their breath this morning. Today is Thursday, December 31, 1999. The news media have been full of dire predictions of the terrible things in store for us in a few hours when midnight strikes.

A small handful of folks are expecting strange supernatural catastrophes to crash down on us with the coming of the millennium. Officials in Israel have expelled some religious fanatics who had gone there to commit suicide at midnight as the millennium arrives in the Holy Land.

It's not some biblical doomsday coming at midnight that worries most people in the developed nations, though. Instead they're waiting anxiously to see what will happen when the date in every computer in the world rolls over, changing from the year 1999 to 2000.

There have been piles of paperbacks and dozens of newspaper articles in the past couple of years warning of the chaos that will break out when all those zeroes start running wild inside our computers. Airplane pilots and air traffic controllers will be staring at blank screens; the power grid in the Northeast will suddenly shut down, plunging our cities into darkness; and water pumping stations will fall silent, leaving us to die of thirst. I saw a picture in yesterday's newspaper of a mother and her children busily filling up hundreds of plastic milk containers with tap water—they have already stockpiled canned goods and toilet paper and who-knows-what-else to prepare for the blow that is about to fall on us all.

I look again at the glass towers across the river. The scene seems peaceful enough. But inside those banks and insurance company offices anxious data-processing people are worrying that tonight will bring the worst of all possible calamities: surprises.

In our technology-based culture surprise is a dirty word. Everything from automobile assembly lines and motor vehicle registration to soybean farming depends on predictability. If a computer program I've written gives me a surprise, that means I've fouled up somewhere. That's why people have been working for years to make sure that the zeroes in our computers won't give us any surprises.

This intense preoccupation with predictability and security is a virtue in computer programming. Unfortunately it doesn't work as a way of life. An obsession with mastery becomes a curse in our relationships with other human beings.

Some people take this approach to religion with equally disastrous results. They create a changeless, risk-free religious system in which, if they just obey all the rules, God has to send them to heaven. No surprises. Guaranteed.

Half a mile away a silver Amtrak train slides out of Newark's Penn Station and, glinting in the sunlight, glides noiselessly across the bridge on its way to New York.

When I came to the monastery at the age of nineteen, I was drawn by a world of wonderful monastic stability and predictability, where nothing is arbitrary or whimsical, and where I could meet the unchanging God of order and comfortable sameness. It turned out that I had only some of it right.

Benedict's practical Roman mind certainly wants the monastery to be an orderly place where public prayer gets prayed on time at regular hours, and members are assigned a definite rank in order of seniority. This kind of predictability must have been particularly welcome in sixth-century Italy as the

Goths were pillaging towns and civil order was falling apart. But there was a hitch: predictability and control are the stuff of mastery, not of intimacy. If Benedict wants a way of life which will help us seek God, and lead us to the goal of intimacy with the Lord, that way of life will have to allow plenty of room for God's surprises.

An elderly man was dying. His wife of sixty years asked him, "What kind of casket do you want?" The old fellow looked at her lovingly and smiled. "Oh, I don't know; surprise me!" If mastery thrives on predictability, intimacy thrives on surprises. It is nourished by spontaneity, and grows best in response to the unplanned and the unforeseen. It suffocates in a world of mechanical routine.

Benedict needed to arrange a world that was strictly regulated and at the same time encouraged spontaneity and freedom; a way of life that was orderly, but never wholly predictable. He knew that even in the best-run community human weakness and mistakes will provide plenty of surprises and exceptions. He had a tremendous reverence for the unforeseen and the uninvited because he realized that it is in those very surprises that we are most likely to find the intimacy with God that we're seeking.

Benedict wouldn't allow daily routine and the careful observance of the letter of the law to degenerate into mindless habit and deadening sameness. On the contrary, he wanted the monastic to cultivate a positive attitude toward surprises, to stay alert for the unexpected, always mindful that God is present everywhere and in every event. He insisted that Christ is going to be found particularly in the people who make the most inconvenient and unpredictable demands on us: the poor, the sick, and the surprise visitor.

When our plans or preferences get derailed, the eyes of faith see this as part of some larger, mysterious pattern, an important opportunity to meet intensely and vividly the One we seek, the God of surprise.

This approach works for me a lot of the time. But I have to confess that sometimes when the chips are down I start to feel like one of those worried computer engineers, afraid that life is about to spring some nasty surprise on me. And when bad things do happen, it can still take me a while to see them as opportunities to meet God.

I'm well down Frank Rodgers Boulevard in Harrison now, dodging the stray drops of water that attack unwary pedestrians walking under the railroad bridge. I wonder: will the trains really stop running at midnight?

For Reflection

1. Read John 2:1–11, the story of the miracle at the wedding feast in Cana. Notice that Mary simply presents her son with what she sees as a problem—they're running out of wine—but she doesn't tell him what to do. By leaving the problem in the hands of Jesus she allows him to perform the first of his signs and one of his most beloved miracles, the changing of water into wine. In what situations are you more likely to tell God exactly what needs to be done? Have you recently taken Mary's approach and simply put a problem in the Lord's hands, saying, "Surprise me!"

2. When was the last time you encountered the God of surprise? Was it pleasant? What did you learn from the experience?

15

Performing Arts Center

World without Walls

It's a celebration in red brick and plate glass, full of curves and angles and architectural surprises. At night it glows in the golden glare of floodlights, its chandeliers twinkling through the great glass façade of its four-story lobby, as tiny white lights glisten in the trees outside on the broad entrance plaza. This afternoon I'm strolling along the wide sidewalk in front of the lobby, checking the colorful posters announcing this month's offerings at NJPAC, the New Jersey Performing Arts Center.

The NJPAC isn't just a center for performances of music, dance and drama—it's a immense picture window opening onto the world's cultures. Here the rich and varied heritage of the whole human family passes in a joyous colorful parade.

This first poster is for Evgeny Kissin, a Russian-born pianist. The next shows the smiling face of Tito Paris, a Cape Verdean artist who sings in Portuguese and Creole. India's Ragamal Music and Dance Theater follows him. Then comes the NDR Symphony Orchestra of Hamburg.

I smile at the memory of a performance of the Polish Youth Symphony I attended here recently, where everyone milling around during intermission was chatting in Polish.

I stroll by the next set of notices, reading as I go: Julio Bocca and the Ballet Argentino. The Balé Folclórico de Bahia from Brazil. Glancing down this line of posters is like taking a quick tour of the world.

The NJPAC is quite at home in Newark, which has been home to people of so many different cultures over the years. The old German and Italian neighborhoods now belong to Portuguese, Filipino, and other groups. Women in Indian saris glide along the sidewalks past shops whose signs are written in Korean or Spanish. Each culture, each person, contributes something unique and irreplaceable to the colorful character of our city. The NJPAC, like Newark itself, has a wide, welcoming embrace that includes folks of every race, culture, and language.

Benedict's vision of a monastery reflects this same openness. The differences that divided people in the Roman world and walled them off from one another disappeared inside the cloister. Ex-slaves stood next to nobles to sing the psalms. Scholars labored alongside illiterates in the monastery kitchen. Converted Goths sat down to eat with former Roman foot soldiers. This conscious acceptance of a wide variety of people as community members carried over naturally into the great monastic virtue of hospitality. Pilgrims, poor people, and guests were to be welcomed as Christ himself.

The last of the glass-covered posters radiates a riot of vivid colors. The distinctive feathered headdresses and unmistakable brilliant Aztec costumes make it easy to guess this one before I can actually read the name. Yup! The Ballet Folklórico de México.

In the Old Testament, openness to strangers is more than some pleasant Semitic custom—it's a central way of encountering God. In Chapter 18 of the book of Genesis, for instance, Abraham welcomes three mysterious guests who later turn out to be divine messengers. The Letter to the Hebrews reminds us, "Do not neglect to show hospitality, for by that means some have entertained angels without knowing it" (Hebrews 13:3). In his chapter on "The Reception of Guests," Benedict quotes Jesus' saying from the Gospel, "I was a stranger and you welcomed me" (Matthew 25:35).

The guest is important to the monastery precisely because he or she is different. Being open to the otherness of others is one way the monastic community leaves itself open to the work of the Spirit. Benedict says this in so many words in Chapter 61, "The Reception of Visiting Monks": "[The visiting monk] may, indeed, with all humility and love make some reasonable criticisms and observations, which the abbot should prudently consider; it is possible that the Lord guided him to the monastery for this very purpose."

Since there is no way to predict just how God is going approach us next, our quest for divine intimacy requires us to always remain open to the widest possible range of people and experiences.

I cross the street to the corner of Military Park, the old training place where the local militia drilled in the late 1600s. From over here you can take in the curved façade of the Performing Arts Center in one glance. Its red brick is meant to evoke the loft buildings and factories that once thrived in this neighborhood. Its wide expanses of plate glass speak of openness to the vast and varied universe that stretches far beyond the boundaries of downtown Newark.

People who are into mastery can't deal with a world that is too wide or too open. They need a universe that's narrow and closed up, small enough for them to manage easily. Anything foreign is a threat.

For certain people religion provides just such a closed system. Whether they are Christian, Jewish, or Muslim, their faith provides a safe haven that protects them from ideas or people that might otherwise challenge their comfortable preconceptions. Their God's heart is a cramped ghetto with room for only one select group of people (who just happen to look and speak like them!). Their fundamentalist faith insulates them the way the safe bottle does a baby crab.

Christians who find this kind of sheltered narrowness in the Gospel are conveniently ignoring the whole message of Jesus' life and death. He broke down the walls of division and prejudice and bigotry, ignoring all of the accepted social and religious barriers that divided people in the Judaism of his day. He talked with women in public, welcomed prostitutes, dined with tax collectors, and touched lepers. It was this attitude of openness to everyone that got Jesus in trouble: "This man welcomes sinners and eats with them!"

Jesus' whole life reveals to the world a God of intimacy whose wide-open heart embraces people of every culture and language and race and social status, inviting them all to share eternal life. The kingdom of heaven, then, must be a wildly colorful kaleidoscope, filled as it is with all of God's beloved children, from Asians to aborigines, from Africans to Eskimos. One contemporary Christian writer suggests that the heavenly table is "open to everyone who's ready to sit down with everyone."

I start to cut across the park toward Trinity Episcopal Church, organized in the 1740s. Its white tower, they say, dates back to 1804.

I begin to wonder if my heart is in fact as wide open as I like to think it is. How good am I, really, at meeting Jesus in every one of the different people I run into each day? Do I limit my search for God to folks I get along with easily, whose personalities or dispositions I enjoy, or whose skin is the same color as mine? How open am I to people who see the world quite differently from me because they're not Catholic, or because they come from a different part of the country or from another culture? When Jesus comes to me as a poor woman at the door or a homeless man begging on the street, does he get the same respect from me as my friends or family do?

The wide-open facade of the NJPAC challenges me to look at my own heart. Like the monastery itself, my heart had better be open wide in grateful welcome to a variety of people, including the stranger and the needy. This is my best chance of meeting the God I'm looking for.

I've crossed Broad Street and started up Central Avenue. Three blocks ahead is old St. Patrick's Pro-Cathedral, built in 1848 by the Irish and German immigrant Catholics. These days you can go to Sunday Mass there in Spanish.

For Reflection

1. Read Matthew 5:43–48, in which Jesus challenges us to love our enemies and not restrict our love just to friends and fellow citizens. Verse 48 is usually translated something like "you must be perfect as your heavenly Father is perfect." The New Jerusalem Bible, however, gets closer to the real sense of the verse with "You must therefore set no bounds to your love, just as your heavenly Father sets none to his."

2. In the Jewish society of Jesus' time there were clearly defined categories of outcasts with whom a pious Jew would not associate, such as prostitutes and other public sinners, Samaritans, tanners, camel drivers, and perfume merchants. Are there groups of people who are outcasts in your life, people you look down on, or about whom you automatically assume the worst? Is there a certain individual who you have made an outcast in your life?

PART FOUR

Keep Heading Homeward

16

Rush Hour

Answering the Call

Tuesday, 8:15 a.m. Rush hour is in full swing. I've joined hundreds of daily commuters dashing across the elevated pedestrian concourse that connects Penn Station Newark with some nearby office towers. Everyone is in a hurry, as if each of us is answering our own urgent, silent summons.

This well-dressed fellow beside me with the fancy leather attaché case and the grim look is, I figure, answering the siren song of power—he probably gets high on making things happen.

Weaving around slower commuters we hurry, five or six abreast, across the wide glass-enclosed bridge toward the Sheraton.

An attractively made-up woman in her early thirties is on my other elbow, a laptop hanging from her shoulder. Hmm…maybe she's responding to the call to prove that she's as good as any of her male co-workers at getting promoted up the corporate ladder.

We swerve smoothly to the left and down the carpeted corridor past the hotel entrance, a restaurant, a book store, a health spa, some fast food shops, an optician's, and several small boutiques.

What about this man plodding dutifully along, wearing a slightly wrinkled suit and a worried expression? What's beckoning him is most likely the hope of financial security for his family.

At the yogurt shop we all swing to our right toward the next glass tube that bridges McCarter Highway.

This gray-haired woman shuffling heavily up ahead seems worn out before the day has even started. She's probably responding to the human instinct for sheer survival, just aiming to get through the day.

I glance up at the high glass towers overhead just as we plunge inside Gateway Two and past a shoeshine stand.

Suddenly snatches from the prologue to the Holy Rule come to mind: "If we wish to dwell in the tent of [God's] kingdom, we will never arrive unless we run there by doing good deeds." I start to picture my fellow monks racing along beside me, four or five abreast. "Run while you have the light of life, that the darkness of death may not overtake you." I can easily recognize each individual monk out of the corner of my eye just by his familiar gait. "If we wish to reach eternal life…we must run and do now what will profit us forever." The youngest brothers are sprinting with the self-assured enthusiasm of youth. "As we progress in this way of life and in faith, we shall run on the path of God's commandments, our hearts overflowing with the inexpressible delight of love." My favorites are the senior members of the house. They've tossed aside their canes and walkers and are setting the pace for the rest of us with the smooth, swift lope of cross-country champions. Their faces glow with a quiet, joyful serenity.

I'm snapped back to the reality of rush hour when I almost collide with two men who stop abruptly to enter a coffee shop. The rest of us keep surg-

ing silently onward past a stationery store and a newspaper stall, each of us still on our own private mission.

I start to realize that for all our differences, everyone in this crowd is responding to the same call deep inside: a nameless longing that keeps us seeking for more. Since the dawn of history different people have been interpreting the invitation of the inner voice in different ways. Many keep mishearing it: they think that their ultimate goal is to acquire possessions or financial security, or to be esteemed or loved—or even feared—by others. They spend their lives desperately chasing after finite things that never quite satisfy them.

A young man in work boots and jeans takes out a tiny cell phone, flips it open, and starts speaking into it without slowing his pace.

Benedict knows that we often have a hard time interpreting our deep inner hunger, so he tries to help us in hastening toward our true goal. Our true goal is not mastery (which is always limited to the here and now) but union with the transcendent One who invites us into an infinite future. Everything in the monastic life, then, is directed somehow toward this final goal of intimacy.

This explains why Christ plays such a central role in the Rule. He is the way to our goal, the one through whom we experience intimacy with God and through whom we are able to share that love with others. We encounter God by encountering Christ in the liturgy, in material things, in the events of daily life, and especially in the people around us. Jesus, "the way, the truth, and the life" (John 14:6), shows us that the way to intimacy with the Father is the way of selfless love, vulnerability, and obedience.

All Christians are called to this search for God. The vowed monastic quest is simply a more radical and more visible way of responding to it. The life of the cloister reminds the rest of the Church in a dramatic way that our true meaning is found not in mastery over creation but in intimacy with God.

A life of humble obedience can remind a world full of power seekers that pulling your own strings or having it your way is not the path to real happiness. A life of vowed frugality and common ownership reminds a world scrambling to accumulate material wealth, "Do not store up for yourself treasures on earth, where moth and decay destroy and thieves break in and steal" (Matthew 6:19). A life of vowed celibacy for the sake of the kingdom may catch the attention of a world in a mad rush after sensual pleasure and superficial relationships, and suggest to it that we are all called to a life of relatedness, not simply on a surface or physical level, but on the deep level of selfless, mutual giving.

The corridor widens and the crowd starts to thin out as we glide on the gray carpet between matching gray walls enlivened by cheerful abstract paintings.

Like any other Christian, I sometimes start running in answer to the wrong call. Maybe I'm being moved by a desire for mastery (to prove something to myself, say, or to earn people's respect). Maybe I'm looking for a false intimacy, a thinly disguised kind of mastery that seeks the shallow gratification of being admired, or manipulates people into caring about me. Sooner or later, though, the Lord's voice will break through the noise again. It may be in something a brother says to me, or a verse of a psalm at Vespers, or some trivial incident, but the call gets through clearly and guides me back in the direction of what Benedict calls "our true home."

Just a final few of us pass the information desk and take the escalator down to the street level lobby where little pushcarts are serving gourmet coffee and overpriced croissants. The race has quieted down now, and the rush has slowed to a purposeful walk.

As I push through the revolving door and out into the cool breeze on Mulberry Street, I whisper a prayer for all my fellow runners this morning: Lord, keep us all on the right path, and don't let any of us grow weary today on our way to the kingdom.

For Reflection

1. In Philippians 1:9–10 Paul writes, "And this is my prayer: that your love may increase ever more and more in knowledge and every kind of perception, to discern what is of value." Later, in Chapter 3, verse 13, he says, "… forgetting what lies behind but straining forward to what lies ahead, I continue my pursuit toward the goal, the prize of God's upward calling, in Christ Jesus." Are there things that you sometimes run after that are not of value, that do not lead you toward the goal?

2. If someone were to watch you as you work, what would they conclude you value most? What would your actions reveal about your real goal in life?

17

Casa dos Presentes

Being a Gift

Mirrors, silverware, china platters, baby clothes, a stainless steel electric coffee maker, linen tablecloths and napkins fill two plate glass windows. The big sign overhead reads *Regalos* (gifts). What a neat place, I think as I walk past. Everything in this store is going to be given by someone as a present! Happy images of birthday parties, weddings, anniversaries, and First Communions start making a joyful collage in my memory as I continue my way up Ferry Street.

The reason we enjoy giving one another gifts is that it's in our very nature: we are made in the image of God the gift-giver. In order to be truly ourselves, then, we have to give ourselves in love the way God does. Doing anything less than this with our lives leaves us unfinished, unsatisfied. The deepest human drama is the struggle to make ourselves into a gift.

A reflection glides slowly across the plate glass—an elderly couple strolling slowly arm in arm, deep in conversation.

There are lots of ways we can make ourselves a gift to others: by carefully preparing a French class, making a quick phone call to a friend who's home sick in bed, or managing a pleasant smile and a cheerful word despite being worried or in a hurry. Preparing a meal for your family, going off to work every day, or taking your son to the park for a game of catch are all ways of making yourself into a gift. Giving yourself to others, the vocation of every Christian, can make you look like an oddball in a world based on self-centered materialism and consumerism.

Two blocks later I'm passing in front of a second gift store, this one is Portuguese—*Casa dos Presentes* (house of gifts). I stop for a moment to enjoy the cheerful display of *presentes*. The window sparkles with silver tea sets, shelves of fancy glassware, and brightly painted platters. The reflection of a number 31 bus glides across a squat silver teapot, curls around a cocktail shaker and, after slithering across the bases of two shiny candlesticks, disappears through the mirror of a jewelry case at the left side of the window.

The mystery of God the giver has another side as well: the Lord, you see, is also the God of infinite acceptance. God accepts each of us as a gift every minute of every day. In our joys and our sorrows, in our silly fits of selfishness, in our passions and our pleasures, in our prayers and our fumbling efforts at intimacy, even in our mistaken chasing after false gods, God is constantly accepting us.

So, to be truly myself, created in the divine image, I have to learn not just to be a gift, but also, like God, to receive other people as gifts. I need to

approach life in a spirit of gratitude, looking at everyone around me, every situation and every event as a gift waiting to be accepted—even when that gift comes in the form of suffering or humiliation.

In my own experience, at least, I find that I'm much more comfortable giving gifts and doing things for others than accepting gifts and letting others do things for me. Some of that, I suppose, comes from my roles of priest and teacher, in which I'm expected to always be doing things for others. Some years ago, though, I got a good taste of what it means to be on the receiving end. After a serious knee operation I had to spend several days in the hospital. Every time I wanted to move into or out of bed I had to call a nurse to hold my foot up so that my knee wouldn't bend. The slightest little twist would send a wave of blinding pain shooting through my whole body. This dependency on others was a real moment of grace, making me rely completely on someone else, literally putting myself in someone else's hands and trusting that they wouldn't let me down. I experienced what it means to receive other people as gifts instead of being a gift to them.

When I accept a gift, when I just let somebody love me, I'm no longer master of the situation. To some degree or other I've left myself vulnerable, open to intimacy. This of course makes no sense to our mastery-centered culture in which the most important thing is to pull your own strings and control things.

A dozen pretty white-and-blue Lladro figurines crowd a glass shelf, each one lost in his or her own world, ignoring the others on either side.

I turn from the window. As I walk I begin thinking about the people who are gifts in my life. Let's see…there's my mother and father, naturally, and my brothers and my sister…my brother monks…my special friends, both men and women.

How fully have I accepted them as gifts, though? Don't I often keep a safe distance, trying to keep control of the situation? If I haven't done too badly sometimes with family and friends, I still have trouble accepting God unconditionally. I keep holding back, hoping to find a way to stay in control while at the same time accepting Christ, the infinite gift.

Before I know it I'm at the corner of Bruen Street.

Lord, I pray silently, let me spend my life giving myself and receiving others and yourself as gifts. May my life help to turn the whole world one day into a Casa dos Presentes, a house of gifts.

For Reflection

1. In Exodus 35:4–29 each Israelite is encouraged to bring some sort of special gift for the furnishing of the new tent of meeting: gold, cloth, skins, dye, jewels, etc. Think of a gift have you been given by the Lord, perhaps one you've discovered only recently. How might you take it to Jesus for the building up of his kingdom? How and for whom might this gift best be put to use right now?

2. Make a list of some of the people you receive as gifts in your life, and ask yourself how each is a gift to you. Then take that same list of people and name the ways in which you are a gift to each of them.

3. At times God gives us something which we don't recognize as a gift because it comes as suffering or pain. Have you ever had a bad experience which you later recognized as a gift from the Lord?

4. Everything you have has been given you by God except one thing—your sins. Jesus wants them. He asks you to hand them over to him to be washed away. Does this seem like a strange gift to give? If there is some particular sin that you're reluctant to lift up to God, ask yourself what's keeping you back. What would it take to get you to give that gift to God?

_18_

Marigolds

Transformation

.

Market Street in the Ironbound section points me straight toward home. I pass a couple of brick apartment buildings, a Portuguese bar and grill, a television repair shop, and a sign maker's. At the corner of Madison there's restaurant called The Titanic. Its sign boasts a picture of a sleek steamship at one end, and the predictable iceberg at the other.

A bright splash of color draws my eye back to the sidewalk. Next to the curb, shimmering pink and gold in the glaring sun, is a big planter full of petunias and marigolds. When I was little I used to plant marigold seeds in a pot on a windowsill each spring and watch awestruck as the first tiny green shoots appeared. Every year I'd stare in wonder as the miracle unfolded once again. First a little white thread would push out of the soil in the shape of an upside-down U, then the next day the white thread had become a fragile stalk with two tiny oval leaves. It was as if some awesome, irresistible force were in the ground, launching the miraculous plant into the world.

Five blocks ahead stand the tall glass towers of downtown. The skyline has changed in recent years as more and more twenty-story buildings have sprouted up: the Gateway complex, the Blue Cross Building, Seton Hall Law School. The Chamber of Commerce boasts about how well the area is developing, and the city's promoters love to talk about growth.

As remarkable as the growth of the downtown area is, it's nothing compared to what happens to marigold seeds. A seed seems like a pretty ordinary thing at first glance: everybody knows that you put it in the ground and water it, and it becomes a flower or a plant. But this simple fact is actually one of nature's deepest mysteries. A seed, you see, doesn't grow. What a seed does is something very different from just getting bigger. Crystals grow, and so do stalagmites in caverns. But crystals and stalagmites, for all their changing and growing, will never be anything but bigger crystals and taller stalagmites. Living things, though, can undergo another very different kind of change. It's called transformation.

Even the youngest child knows the difference between growth and transformation. No one ever thinks of an oak tree as an overgrown acorn, or looks at a daisy and says "Oh! Look at the big seed!" A daisy happens because a seed stops being a seed. An oak tree happens only when some acorn, buried in the cold, dark earth, stops being an acorn and bursts open, becoming something new.

The purpose of a marigold seed, then, is to stop being a seed and be transformed into a flower. A tadpole gives up being a tadpole so it can become a frog. A caterpillar whose life's goal is to master being a caterpillar by becoming the biggest, fattest, furriest caterpillar in the world is missing the whole reason for its existence, and is sure to end up a very frustrated little creature. The caterpillar has to be transformed, to die to its feet and its pretty fur. Only when it does this will its life finally make sense—when a gorgeous new butterfly floats on the summer breeze.

I'm startled to find myself still standing in the middle of the sidewalk staring at the pot of marigolds. I look around, hoping that no one has been watching me, and decide to move along.

The mystery of transformation is at the very heart of Christian spirituality: what's true of caterpillars, seeds, tadpoles, and acorns is true of me as well. Jesus never calls me to be a better Christian, never challenges me to improve, to become holier or more saintly. He certainly never asks me to grow. No, but he does keep calling me over and over to be transformed. In fact he even phrases the challenge in terms of a seed: "Unless the grain of wheat falls to the earth and dies, it remains just a grain of wheat" (John 12:24).

It's clear enough that a seed is meant to be transformed into a marigold, and a tadpole into a frog. But what does Jesus expect me to turn into? Saint

Basil of Caesaria answers with startling simplicity: "A human being is a creature whose purpose is to become God." The goal of my existence is to be transformed into Christ. Paul puts it to the Galatians, "It is no longer I that live, but Christ that lives in me " (Galatians 2:20). Just as a marigold seed's existence has no meaning until the seed at last turns into a marigold, my life makes no real sense until I finally become changed into Christ.

As I cross Madison Street I notice scraggly blades of grass and scruffy weeds along the curb and in the cracks in the sidewalks, wherever stray seeds have found enough soil. I've never paid much attention to them before, but this afternoon they remind me of the true meaning of my life, of my call to be transformed.

The world keeps offering substitutes for this transformation; and often enough, enthralled with the glitter of possessions, power, and prestige, we fall for them. "If I just had a lot of money, that's all I'd need." "If I could be in complete control of things, then life would be perfect." "If people just respected me more and appreciated me, my life would be complete."

My true destiny, though, calls me far beyond such a limited world of created things and human power. I'm made for intimacy and infinity. The psalmist sings, "My soul and body cry out for the living God." But this destiny comes at a price, because the rules for transformation apply to me, too. If the caterpillar has to say good-bye to its fur, and the tadpole has to leave behind its sleek shape, then I have to let go of my false self, my preoccupying projects, and especially of my mastery approach to living.

I pass the car wash where a line of perfectly clean-looking cars are waiting their turn to be scrubbed and polished. Alongside the busy Burger King I notice a few more of those tiny weeds in the cracks in the pavement.

Unlike transformation in the world of nature, though, being transformed into Christ is a process that takes a whole lifetime of continual, radical, ongoing conversion. Every single day my false self has to undergo dozens of deaths. A co-worker makes a cutting remark to me, but I realize that she's having a terrible time with her teenager these days so I just let it go instead of lashing back. My nine-year-old daughter reminds me that I promised to take her roller skating—there goes the quiet afternoon I'd planned! I have a phone message asking me to call back an overly talkative friend; I know it's going to cost me an hour, but I pick up the phone and dial anyway.

The process of dying to myself won't be complete until I enter the life that lies beyond my earthly existence and I'm fully transformed into Christ.

I'm in the noisy darkness where Market Street passes under the train station. Squinting toward the bright scene at the other end of the underpass I can make out beds of flowers glowing in the sunshine beside the Gateway building. The folks waiting at the bus stop stand, evenly spaced, in a neat straight line.

I used to plant my marigolds in a row like that.

For Reflection

1. "Unless the grain of wheat falls to the ground and dies it remains just a grain of wheat" (John 12:24). Has some person or a situation ever asked you to die to yourself? What did you do? How did it feel?

2. "For me, to live is Christ" (Philippians 1:21). Can you think of someone who truly seems to have been transformed into Christ? Can you sense what it may have cost them?

3. The false self offers resistance to the Spirit's call to transformation. How does this resistance usually show up in your life? Is there anything you can do to overcome this resistance besides pray?

19

The Immigration Office

Moving On

Trying not to stare, I glance discreetly at their faces. A few are worried, and others are weary with years of struggle and suffering. Most of them, though, are calm and relaxed. The long, single-file line stretches for two blocks along Walnut Street to the front door of the INS building—the U.S. Immigration and Naturalization Service.

Men and women of various ages are standing on the sunny sidewalk, some sitting on the edge of the long, low planters that run along the front of the Federal Courthouse. I exchange an occasional nod or a smile as I pass by, and try to guess their nationalities by listening for a telltale scrap of conversation in some foreign tongue. A murmured word of Spanish...a snatch of Brazilian Portuguese...then something that sounds like Russian.

This afternoon I'm struck by how different my situation is from theirs. Although all of us from around the world are sisters and brothers in one human family, I'm different in one important way: I was born just seven blocks down the street—I am home.

The line turns left up the wide stone steps into the INS offices. Suddenly I remember going up those stairs some years ago with one of my students. He had asked me to come with him to the Immigration office when he was filing for political asylum from an Eastern European country.

What must it be like for the people on this line who are emigrating from their homes? They have to let go of their whole existence, leave behind everything that's familiar and dear, and move to a strange new land the way Abraham did in the Bible.

Our sense of mastery is based on familiarity with our environment and on knowing pretty much what to expect in any given situation. This comes home to me in a humorous way every time I take city kids to camp overnight in the middle of the woods. Some teenage boys who are perfectly at home on a city street at 3 a.m. are terrified at being in this strange new place full of unknown threats and mysterious sounds. Their street survival skills are useless in the forest. They're not at home.

There are times when life naturally challenges me to pull up stakes and leave the comfortable security of what I know in favor of something new and strange, whether that's going off to the first day of kindergarten or college, or moving to a different job in another city.

Sometimes the call to move on is subtle, maybe just a nagging sense that something is missing in my life, or a remark that a friend made that leaves me unsettled deep inside. Sometimes a tragic upheaval leaves me no choice—the death of a family member, the loss of a job, or a medical emergency lands me in the middle of some strange new wilderness.

A man and a woman walk slowly out of the door and down the steps, engrossed in reading a blue slip of paper they're holding between them.

For a Christian, getting uprooted is far more than just one of life's normal inconveniences—it's a special opportunity for intimacy with God. It's the Lord calling me to let go of whatever I may be hanging on to, to say good-bye to familiar territory, and to move on in hope into the wilderness. As the Israelites found out, though, the desert can be terrifying. Life is precarious there, and you have to depend on God for everything: water, food, protection from enemies, and guidance in the trackless waste.

In the spiritual life such an uprooting is called a conversion experience. Something so forceful and unexpected happens to me that my usual ways of thinking, feeling, and acting are completely turned around. Moses meets God in the burning bush (Exodus 3:10), and Saul is struck blind after encountering the risen Jesus on the road to Damascus (Acts 9:1–19), and neither man is ever again what he was before. They have been called into a totally new and unfamiliar place. For a Christian the experience of loss and upheaval is an invitation to enter more deeply into the paschal mystery—it is Christ's call to closer intimacy with him.

A couple of men stand near the entrance handing out little handbills and calling out "Immigration photos, *fotografias*," trying to steer business to a nearby storefront.

There is, however, a crucial difference between spiritual conversion and the experience of the folks on the immigration line who are coming to a new land: many of these immigrants hope one day to become citizens and settle here for good. They'll put down roots and raise their children as Americans. But spiritual conversion doesn't work like this. I don't have one big conversion experience and then take up residence in the new land undisturbed for the rest of my life. The radical letting go that I'm called to is more than a one-time event—it's a way of life. I keep pulling up stakes and moving forward in an ongoing, constantly renewed journey. Life is a continuous adventure in intimacy in which I'm constantly being asked to respond anew to the Lord who keeps calling me out into yet one more desert.

This is why Benedict's vision of the monastic life is so tremendously dynamic. Convinced that Christ reveals himself to us every day in people and events, Benedict arranges everything to help us to keep watching and listening for a God who is always calling us to conversion. The Rule prescribes that each day should begin with the chanting of Psalm 95 because of the verse, "If today you hear his voice, harden not your hearts."

Despite its calm, repetitive cycle of prayer and work, and the seemingly static security of the vow of stability, the monastery is not a place to go to find a comfortable niche and hunker down spiritually. It's a place for people who are constantly on the way somewhere in response to the Divine invitation, and is spiritually much more like a tent than a castle.

As I start across Broad Street, leaving behind the long line of immigrants, I notice a long strip of white canvas stretching across the front of an apartment building ahead. In bright blue letters it gently taunts harried commuters: "If you lived here, you'd be home now!" I smile, picturing the banner that we could hang on our monastery. In big blue letters it would proclaim, "If you lived here, you still wouldn't be home."

Reaching the other curb just as the light changes, I picture another banner, this one encircling the whole globe at the equator. Someone on the moon could easily read its bright blue message: "If you lived here, you still wouldn't be home."

For Reflection

1. Read Genesis 12, which begins with the Lord's command to Abram, "Go forth from the land of your kinsfolk and from your father's house to a land that I will show you." When has the Lord asked you to leave a familiar situation and move on into a strange new land— whether geographically or psychologically or spiritually? How did you react to the moving? Who chose the place you are in right now? God? You? Someone else?

2. After God had brought the Israelites out of Egypt and into the wilderness, they began to long for the good old days back in the brickyards. There are many passages in the books of Exodus, Numbers, and Deuteronomy that make up the murmuring traditions. "We remember the fish we used to eat without cost in Egypt, and the cucumbers, the melons, the leeks, the onions and the garlic. But now we are famished; we see nothing before us but this manna (Numbers 11:5–6)." Have you ever complained to God about a new place you'd been taken to? Did you eventually come to realize that it was a place of new life for you? How did it affect your relationship of intimacy with God?

3. "If you lived here, you wouldn't be home." How do your attitudes or actions tell others that your real home is elsewhere?

20

The Funeral Procession

The Web of Intimacy

I sense it somehow even before looking down at the street—that strange, solemn hush that always happens when a funeral procession is passing.

From the top step I scan the line of traffic stopped in front of the monastery. Sure enough, the cars all have their headlights on, and each has a little purple "Funeral" flag stuck by a magnet onto its hood. A biting icy wind spins the first few tiny flecks of snow across the early afternoon grayness as I head down the stone steps to start my walk.

I stroll quickly down the hill toward the traffic light that has momentarily halted the funeral procession. As I come alongside the hearse I start to wonder about the man in the coffin. How old was he? Did he have a big family? What did he do for a living? Did he know he was dying?

I glance at the solemn-faced mourners in the cars and wonder who they might be. Probably his wife and children in the limousine. Then some other relatives and close friends. The rest, I suppose, are co-workers and neighbors who took the day off to say good-bye to their friend.

For him the struggle between mastery and intimacy is now over. What is left

95

is the love between him and his wife and his children, the caring concern he had for his close friends, and the bond of affection with fellow workers. Far from ending, these relationships have become woven forever into the web of intimacy that spans the boundary between this life and the next. Some of us are still on the earthly end of the web, but lots of others have already moved on to the eternal part. Our departed family members and friends, our mothers and fathers in the faith, ancestors who never even knew us, all are joined to us in love by the communion of saints. Paul puts it another way: we're all members of the body of Christ (1 Corinthians 12:12, ff.).

In some Christian cultures families go to the cemetery on a certain day each year to have a picnic at the grave of their deceased relatives, reaffirming and strengthening the bonds that still connect all of them, the living and the departed. For these people death is not a drop through a trapdoor into oblivion but a passing from one kind of presence to another.

The traffic starts to move, and the hearse glides smoothly away, taking with it the eerie silence and the train of cars with their little purple flags.

"Always keep death before your eyes," Benedict advises in Chapter 4 of the Rule. This advice is not as morbid as it may seem at first. He's not asking me to philosophize about the phenomenon of death in general, but to remind myself constantly of the solemn fact that one day my own life as I know it is going to end. This helps keep me focused on a solemn and certain truth: my real goal lies in the realm of eternal loving intimacy with God, and not in the mastery of this passing world.

Nothing points up the contrast between intimacy and mastery more clearly than the experience of growing old and dying.

When I'm a young adult, much of my life is concerned with mastery: I establish a family and a career, I set goals for myself and maybe even a timetable for accomplishing them. I define myself in terms of my competencies and skills, and draw justifiable satisfaction from my achievements.

Then, inevitably, unsettling little signs start showing themselves at some point. I notice my receding hairline. I attend my high school reunion and gasp at how old all of my classmates have gotten. Friends and I start joking about bifocals and AARP discounts.

The rough hand of the wind gives me a rude shove from behind. I tighten my scarf around my neck and tug my knitted cap down over my ears. Winter is setting in.

To the extent that I have defined myself mostly in terms of mastery, the normal diminishment of my mental and physical abilities comes as a terrible loss, and death is just the ultimate pie-in-the-face. Everything I am and have is slowly wrested away from me—control, consciousness, life itself—until I'm dragged down kicking and screaming into the dark unknown. Death and mastery are sworn enemies in a battle which death always wins.

But if I've been following Benedict's advice and living life as if it were about intimacy and not mastery, then the inexorable march of advancing years and even death itself take on a deep and beautiful meaning: they are part of the triumph of the cross of Christ. As a Christian I believe that my suffering and dying are my share in the suffering and dying of Jesus, and that through his rising from the dead I will one day rise to life and to eternal oneness with God and be reunited with all the loved ones who have gone before me.

The procession is already out of sight when I reach the corner and turn to head down the hill. On Branford Place a driver slows and greets me with two quick beeps. I can barely make out a gloved hand waving inside the dark car, but can't see who it is. I wave back just to be friendly. The snow is starting to fall in a furious sideways rush. I pick up my pace.

"Life is changed not ended," says the preface for the Mass of Christian Burial. Life, which on Earth inevitably involves struggles with mastery, is transformed into pure intimacy in heaven. I think of it this way: some day, whether I like it or not, Sister Death will come and shatter the protective bottle of my mastery project. She will set me free from the prison of my compulsions and preoccupations and lay me open at last to the love of the One who has been pursuing me all my life. The story of God's love for me will finally be complete. Intimacy will no longer demand risk and struggle and courage but will be sheer delight, unspeakable joy with the risen Lord and with all the saints forever.

I shove my hands deeper into my jacket pockets. This is going to be a wintry walk, long and cold.

For Reflection

1. Read the famous hymn about Christ's emptying himself in Colossians 2:5–11, which reads in part, "He emptied himself, taking the form of a slave…he humbled himself, becoming obedient unto death." Each of our own losses and diminishments is part of Christ's diminishment and self-emptying. When and how have you experienced diminishment in your life? Is mastery more important to you than it was five or ten years ago? How might your different experiences of loss help you to learn about intimacy as you grow older?

2. Read 1 Corinthians 12:12, ff.: "As a body is one though it has many parts, and all the parts of the body, though many, are one body, so also Christ." Reflect on your own intimacy network that spans time and space, and picture the long line of nameless believers who had a part in handing on the faith to you over the centuries. A great-great-great grandmother, for example, who suffered through the death of a newborn baby but held fast to her trust in God and passed that trust on to her other children. What kind of connections, if any, do you sense with these people who have gone before you? Are you eager to meet or be reunited with any particular one of them?